THE DECLARATION
OF INDEPENDENCE

Da Capo Press Reprints in

AMERICAN CONSTITUTIONAL AND LEGAL HISTORY

GENERAL EDITOR: LEONARD W. LEVY

Claremont Graduate School

THE DECLARATION
OF INDEPENDENCE

An Interpretation
and an Analysis

By Herbert Friedenwald

New Introduction By Carl Ubbelohde,
Case-Western Reserve University

DA CAPO PRESS · NEW YORK · 1974

Library of Congress Cataloging in Publication Data

Friedenwald. Herbert. 1870-1944.
    The declaration of independence, an interpretation
and an analysis.

    (Da Capo Press reprints in American constitutional
and legal history)
    Reprint of the 1904 ed. published by Macmillan,
New York.
    Bibliography: p.
    1. United States. Declaration of independence.
I. Title.
E221.F89   1974   973.3'13'072   77-166325
ISBN 0-306-70230-4

INTRODUCTION

Half-way through his work on the Declaration
of Independence, Herbert Friedenwald confides to
his readers his awareness of the inherent pitfalls of
his labor: "No part of the writing of history," he
asserts, "is more difficult than that which aims to
put ourselves in the place of the men participating
in great historic movements, and to attempt to
view the results of their achievements from their
own attitude of mind, to penetrate the well-
springs of their motives. Yet, he continues,
"unless this be undertaken, no substantially correct results can be achieved."[1] Applying this
general stricture to his own effort, Friedenwald
states his intention to analyze and interpret the
Declaration of Independence " . . . not in terms of
twentieth century philosophy or politics, but from
the standpoint of the men who had a share in the
events from which the Declaration arose, and of
which it was, to an extent, the outward
expression."[2]

It is easy to scan those words and miss their
substance. For Herbert Friedenwald, they constituted a testament of faith in his chosen craft and
in his specific objective to publish this study, his

INTRODUCTION

first and only monograph on early American history. To put himself "in the place of the men participating in great historic movements;" to see the Declaration of Independence "from the standpoint of the men who had a share in the events from which" it sprang—these were the natural, perhaps the expected endeavors for a scholar who had travelled the academic and professional paths Friedenwald chose. After graduating at age twenty from The Johns Hopkins University in his native city of Baltimore, Friedenwald began graduate studies in history at the University of Pennsylvania. In 1894 that university awarded him the second doctorate in its history. His dissertation was a study of "The Bounty System of the American Revolution Previous to the Declaration of Independence."[3]

From his academic training Friedenwald gained the intellectual tools of the historian: the technique of searching for and examining historical evidence, the skill of analysis and interpretation of data, and the method of reporting results of his investigations. His professional competence was enhanced particularly in the years from 1897 to 1900 when he held the position as the first superintendent (chief) of the reorganized Manuscript Division of the Library of Congress.[4] A happy blend of scholar and curator resulted.

Friedenwald continued to extend his graduate
school interest in the history of the American
Revolution and as keeper of manuscripts, gained
increasing awareness of the necessity for basing
historical analysis on valid evidence. Four years
after he left the Library of Congress he published
this volume, the earliest major monograph on the
Declaration of Independence by an academically
trained historian.

On first glance Friedenwald's book appears to
be a curiously bifurcated study. The first part
(Chapters I through VI) are constructed in a narrative fashion. They describe the events of the
years from 1774 to July, 1776, and afford the
author the opportunity to interpose his analysis
and interpretation of those events as he fashions
his text chronologically. The second half of the
book (Chapters VII through IX) is static, descrip-
tive and altogether different in tone and purpose.
In the first half of the book Friedenwald writes
about the political act of declaring independence;
in the second, he considers the Declaration of Independence as a document.[5]

The topics Friedenwald considers in the second
part of the volume—the purpose and the
philosophy of the Declaration, its literary merits,
its critics, historical explanations for the "facts
submitted to a candid world"—to a greater or

lesser degree have all been examined with more
detail and sophistication since Friedenwald's time.
It is the first part of the book, and extensions of its
arguments into the second half, that remain
particularly challenging, and worthy of serious
consideration by every student of the American
Revolution. Scholars who came to take up the
Declaration as a topic for study after him have not
quarreled with the validity of his effort. In 1922
Carl Becker would assert that ". . . during the
Revolution, as a matter of course, men were
chiefly interested in the fact that the colonists had
taken the decisive step of separating from Great
Britain; the practical effect of taking this step, at
this time, rather than the form, or even the
substance, of the Declaration itself, was what
chiefly engaged their attention . . . Those who
were ready for *a* declaration of independence
readily accepted *the* Declaration of Independence."[6] And Philip F. Detweiler, writing
forty years after Becker, explained: "To the men
of 1776, unlike those of later generations, the Declaration was news—news more critical than most
of them had ever heard. When the Declaration
was first promulgated, it was widely printed and
distributed, and we may assume that the majority
of Americans heard or read the preamble. But
that was not the part which made it newsworthy.

Attention centered upon the conclusion—the announcement of independence: 'That these United
Colonies are, and of Right ought to be, Free and
Independent States.'"[7]

A quarter-century earlier interest in the Declaration of Independence had run high as the nation
celebrated the centennial of its birth. For years
collectors had gathered autographs of the
"signers." Such patriotic and antiquarian uses of
the history of the Declaration are interesting but
only tangentially related to the purposes Friedenwald had in mind. In the years immediately preceding the publication of this book, Moses Coit
Tyler published his still-valuable essay originally
entitled "The Declaration of Independence in the
Light of Modern Criticism," later incorporated in
The Literary History of the American Revolution.[8] Friedenwald would borrow (with credit)
generously from Tyler. But Tyler had directed his
study to the literary substance of the document.
Friedenwald had embarked on another purpose.[9]

To study the political act of declaring independence, Friedenwald needed to examine the history of the Continental Congress, the agency that
had proclaimed the act of divorce. His analysis of
the structure and work of the Congress convinced
him, as stated in the preface to his book, that
there was "a close interrelation between the

development of the authority and jurisdiction of the Continental Congress and the evolution of the sentiment for independence."[10] This interrelationship is the thread Friedenwald traces in the first part of his book. As the movement for independence drew closer and closer to its climax, the "authority and jurisdiction" of Congress mounted higher and higher and in early July, 1776, the zenith of congressional authority was reached at the moment of the birth of the Republic.

In his analysis of the Continental Congress as a dynamic, federalizing agency, Friedenwald employs a three-tiered construct: (a) the Congress; (b) the committees—within which term are encompassed all the revolutionary, *de facto* agencies of local control, including committees of safety, provincial conventions and congresses; all the instruments through which the American cause was forwarded; and (c) the "people." The relationships each of these bore to the others, and the shifts and changes in those interrelationships, form the substance of his interpretation of the coming of American independence. The reader is constantly returned to the essential pattern—a three-stepped ladder from "people" through "committees" to Congress.

Fittingly, since his purpose is to demonstrate the accretion of power by the Continental

Congress as a concomitant to the drive for separation from the British Empire, Friedenwald introduces the reader to the First Continental Congress (Chapter I). This later allows him a platform on which he demonstrates the growth in congressional authority as the crisis between the colonies and Great Britain deepened. But even here, dyanamic change is in evidence as the author compares the 1774 Congress with the only other voluntary intercolonial gathering like it—the Stamp Act Congress of 1765. By exhibiting distinctions between the 1765 and 1774 meetings, Friedenwald is able to show concisely the progress of the imperial quarrel. The Stamp Act Congress directed petitions asserting the colonists' grievances to the two houses of the British Parliament; the 1774 Congress addressed its petition to the King alone, scorning the legislative body whose authority it was contesting. The balance in argument between economic policy, on the one hand, and natural and constitutional rights, on the other, that had characterized the literary efforts during the Stamp Act crisis was replaced by 1774 with almost total emphasis on American rights. The rhetoric of the assertions had become more strident. Finally, and most significantly, a vital difference occurred in the method by which delegates were chosen to attend the two congresses. In 1765 the men who met in New York had been selected by regularly constituted provincial assemblies; in 1774 the Philadelphia delegates from seven of the twelve represented colonies owed their appointments and were responsive to revolutionary committees.

Of course there was no direct link between the Stamp Act Congress and the First Continental Congress, nor does Friedenwald assert that there was. But his comparison of the two meetings graphically demonstrates the changes that had come in colonial thought and deed in the nine intervening years. And, by the time the 1774 Congress adjourned after resolving to reconvene in the following spring if satisfactory redress of the American grievances had not been attained, the basic instruments for Friedenwald's analysis can be identified—the Congress, the committees, and the "people." At this stage in his discussion, his instruments are rather one-dimensional. The Congress appears basically unfragmented; the "opposition" (the Tories) are said to exist but in a disorganized manner. The committees seem as lacking in division as the Congress and the "people" as much or more so.[11] But this state of affairs does not last long. After the adjournment of the first congress, a regular work assignment had been provided for the committees: the enforcement of the Continental Association. And, with the three-level apparatus now in place and operative, the "people," through their provincial committees, began to experience the application of the congressional agreement.

The committees were the vehicle through which the Continental Congress may be said to have had a popular foundation. In the layered arrangement, the "people" found their voice articulated through the *ad hoc* revolutionary agencies and it was these committees, in turn, who chose and directed the delegates who sat in the general congress. The route was a two-way street: "The Congress and the local committees bore to each other relations of interdependence; the committees created the congress, and the Congress in turn looked to the committees to enforce its recommendations."[12] What intrigued Friedenwald, as it has interested other historians, is the effectiveness of the "arm" or "sanction" extended through these committees. From enforcing the Articles of Association, through preparing military defenses, to support of the war itself after the commencement of hostilities in April, 1775, the "people's" loyal support of the local committees and their work expanded in direct relationship with the evolutionary growth of those extra-constitutional agencies. And the willingness to follow the committees reflected the popular acceptance of the Congress and its works.

As the quarrel with Great Britain deepened, the role of the Congress greatly expanded. In the fall of 1774, the coming together of the first congress and its petitioning for the colonists' redress of grievances and erecting a common boycott of trade, had seemed unusual, even radical. Then, within the short, telescoped time-span of a few months, Congress faced and accepted the responsibilities of adopting, officering, feeding, and directing the Cambridge army encircling General Gage and the British troops in Boston. Money had to be raised; there was a war to fight. "The Congress thus grew, from an impotant body with vague powers designed at first to prepare petitions and addresses, into one having practically complete control of the affairs of a people engaged in a war of revolution, with all that such control implies . . . this evolution is the most important civil and political phenomenon of the period. . . . "[13] A civil and political phenomenon? Yes. But Friedenwald uses the word *phenomenon* in a scientific, not a philosophic sense. He believes the observed situation can be explained, and offers some suggestions.

The able and wise men who sat in the Congress understood the necessity of moving the continent

in the general direction the "people" indicated
(through their local committees) they desired, but
the Congress had to pace itself so as not to be too
much ahead, nor too far behind, the common
mood. The "people," broadly educated over the
past decade by the pamphlet writers and
spokesmen for American rights, could accept each
new step taken by the Congress as an inevitable,
necessary step demanded to protect the common
cause against the relentless encroachments of an
increasingly coercive mother state. But, as the
summer of 1775 waned, and hopeful expectations
of an acceptable reply to the last (Olive Branch)
petition to the King evaporated, the Congress and
the "people" began to face the final question: If
American rights could not be recovered within the
Empire, should separation then become the objective of the struggle? When the time came to ask
that question seriously both the people and the
Congress became increasingly divided.

Now, belately but helpfully, Friedenwald
describes the divisions within the revolutionary
group; his earlier, simpler description of a Whig-
Tory dichotomy is insufficient to indicate the state
of the community. A minimum of three divisions
of the "people" needs to be noted: the Tories,
who were willing to accept the British definition
of the proper constitutional posture of the

provinces within the Empire and who thus opposed the Congress, the committees, and all; the
Conservative Whigs who had worked for
American rights within the Empire but who drew
back from the idea of separating the colonies from
the parent state; and the more Radical Whigs
who came to accept independence as the only solution possible and who became impatient to move
toward the act. (This denomination of groupings,
no less than Friedenwald's use of the term "the
democracy" to describe the followers of the more
Radical Whigs, is imperfect, but it seems foolish
to ignore or to refuse to analyze factions in the
American community because of the difficulty in
finding appropriate names for them.)

It was "the democracy," guided by the Radical
Whig leaders—those willing to get on with the
business of separating the colonies from the
Empire—whom Friedenwald asserts Congress relied on the fostered. In Chapter IV, "The
Congress and the Democracy," he suggests both
an ideological and a partisan basis for the
grouping. These men had not only accepted the
rhetoric of the defenders of American rights; they
were ready to act upon it and in directions both
external and internal. It was, says Friedenwald,
what one would expect " . . . when the people at
large had been fed for ten years and more

upon . . . a diet [of natural rights] and, moreover, were called upon to enlist and fight for the rights which they had been led to believe were theirs, what [was] more natural than they should demand their full share when the time came for distribution?"[14] What distribution? The distribution of governing powers in the new states to be created. Indeed, why should one assume, as some recent students of the American Revolution have done, that the colonists were capable of applying abstract ideas concerning their rights to the imperial quarrel, but unable or willing to translate those abstractions into assumptions concerning their local situations, much nearer and probably (for most colonists) more vital to their interests? And surely, among the components of their local situation, nothing except the course of the war itself could have been as vital as the forthcoming "distribution."

Friedenwald argues that the "time for distribution" and the moment of separation from the Empire bore interesting relationships to each other. The casting off of royal government in America would necessitate more permanent arrangements for governing society than the existing *ad hoc* committees then directing affairs in the colonies. When the time came to replace those older forms there would be disagreement as to

what new arrangements to institute, even among
those united in their opposition to British policies
and the defense of American rights. Those
disagreements, and the attitudes, hopes, and fears
underlying them, led some of the colonies in the
autumn of 1775 to impede progress toward
separation in the Congress by binding their delegates with instructions not to vote for independence. In those provinces where the group
Friedenwald denotes "the aristocracy"—that is,
the Conservative Whigs—controlled the committees or the still regularly structured colonial
assemblies, the opposition to independence can be
explained by the fear of the effect of the "distribution" upon their own continued control of
events.

No claims for the originality of the idea should
be attempted. Friedenwald's citations acknowledge his acceptance of Charles Lincoln's
analysis of the revolutionary movement in Pennsylvania and of Carl Becker's interpretation of
New York politics.[15] If such classification is
helpful, Herbert Friedenwald may be termed a
"progressive" historian, writing about an
"internal revolution." He accepts and explains
the proposition that domestic convulsions accompanied the movement for separating the American
colonies from the British Empire; that "the

contest for independence, in its later stages, that is just before July 4, 1776, in Pennsylvania, New Jersey, North and South Carolina, and to almost an equal extent in New York, Delaware, and Maryland became virtually not less one between the people and the aristocrats for control, than one between the United Colonies and Great Britain for the establishment of a separate government."[16]

To evaluate Friedenwald's thesis requires examination into what might be called the "Idea of Independence," particularly as it manifested itself in the months from late autumn, 1775, to July, 1776. Historians have approached the problem from a variety of assumptions, intent on discovering patterns common to the colonies that might explain both the enthusiasm and the reluctance apparent in the debates on independence. Geographical and sectional factors, both intercolonial and intracolonial, have been called into use; class—economic and social—has been employed as a key; plain practical partisan politics has been applied. In a recent, imaginative effort, John M. Head has suggested that cultural and institutional homogenity, or lack thereof, within a colony, along with economic conditions, actual or potential, may provide the best explanation for the fact that some colonies eagerly pushed for separation, others opposed them.[17]

XX   INTRODUCTION

Eventually, perhaps, an interpretation will be commonly accepted. In the meantime, a student of the Revolution might well consider Head's assertion that, on the matter of independence, each "individual delegate formulated his position in terms of his own personal history."[18] How did an individual, congressional delegate or not, react at the time to the idea of independence?

The idea of independence surely was a more complex concept than the idea of reconciliation. So long as readjustment of imperial relationships was the goal, then, presumably, men could see the future as closely related to the past. Once the unfortunate disarrangements of the last decade were corrected, there would be a return to things as they had been. Conversely, independence pointed in a quite different direction, toward a new and unknown future.

As the American colonists lived through the months from late 1775 to early summer, 1776, the road to reconciliation became more and more clogged with debris, less passable, with each month. Finally it would become completely impassable. Ahead now were only two choices: a retreat to Toryism or a moving toward separation. Presumably every man, as a prophet of his own and his country's future, peered toward independence and saw what his status, experience, education, and philosophic temperment allowed him to see. The view ahead, for almost all men, must have been a mixed scene, in which hopes and fears were intermingled. If, on balance, the hopes prevailed over the fears, then a man could move with some degree of optimism and enthusiasm toward the final act, a declaration of independence for the United Colonies. But if the fears prevailed over the hopes, then the recourse must have been to attempt withdrawal, perhaps neutrality, or, eventually, joining the ranks of the Tories.

In days of quiet calm, with only normal interruptions, men might have considered the question with detachment and reason. But the first six months of 1776 were explosive months, and with war expanding around them men came to the climax of the long debate in an atmosphere that precluded a laboratory-setting for consideration of the eventful question. Each day brought new determinants as the news from the army, from the neighboring colonies, and from England shifted the dimensions and mixed the elements men combined to find their personally-judged answer. In aggregate, the questions they asked of the present and future, and their answers to them, would place them on one side or the other of the line between accepting or rejecting the idea of independence. Those questions were many and varied, but among them the following probably were most significant.

Is a military victory possible? Once the Americans had declared their goal to be separation from the British Empire, bringing their objective in the struggle into harmony with what official British pronouncement had long claimed to be the "rebels" goal, the task ahead was certain to be more arduous than merely defending against British measures to the point where negotiation and reconciliation were achieved. Few men could be deceived by the pleasant prospect of early summer, 1776, when, after the March redemption of Boston, the Americans " . . . were still in complete control of the colonies." [10] Even as the delegates in Philadelphia debated the Declaration, General William Howe would disembark a massive military force at Staten Island and the months ahead promised extensive and hazardous campaigning.

Closely tied with the question of military success was the concomitant query: will foreign aid be necessary? If Great Britain, with her sizeable advantage in population and resources, already had purchased German mercenaries to augment her army, was it not a sign that the Americans, almost innocent of manufacturing and with little more than a symbol of a navy, needed aid from

and perhaps even alliance with France or Spain?
On the answer, negative or affirmative, to that
question hinged a series of dependent questions: Is
foreign aid or an alliance obtainable? Will the
price be so high as to make the purchase unwise?
And, particularly, can substantial aid or an
alliance be secured without first declaring independence? Or would France or Spain refuse the
quantity of aid needed, or an alliance, until the
colonists clearly and demonstratively proved their
intentions by announcing separation from the
British Empire?

Mostly all of the men who were called, or who
called themselves "Whigs" in 1776 agreed that
whether separation or reconciliation was the goal,
a more permanent union of the American colonies
was needed. Something more formally structured
than the Continental Congress would be required
either for negotiating and maintaining a settlement with the Mother Country or for
embarking upon life as a sovereign, independent
nation. But as the question of independence
shifted focus, and men differed in their response to
it, they also responsed differently to the question
whether confederation should come before or after
separation. Radical Whigs argued that to delay
separation until a constitutional federation had
been perfected would so jeopardize chances for a

military victory that the cause would be lost.
Others believed that only the unrelenting
pressures of the emergency could provide the impetus that would persuade the colonists to overcome the centrifugal sentiments and draw together
into a federal republic; that once independence
was declared it would be impossible to gain
agreement on federation.

There were both pessimistic and optimistic
responses to the question whether it would be
possible to erect a republic government over such
an extensive area as that encompassed by the
revolting colonies. The differences in religion, the
rivalries over land claims, the disputes concerning
boundaries, the suspicions and jealousies among
the colonies seemed to some men too great an im-
pediment to hope to overcome. Others believed,
despite the obvious hurdles, that there was more
than would bring the colonies together than would
drive them apart. A vision of a contiguous,
continental American "empire" rose up to lure
these men on toward independence.

What about economic survival? Would it be
possible outside of the British Empire? Would
separation enhance or diminish trade and commerce and, eventually, manufacturing, and not
just for the current effort of the war but in the
decades and for generations to come? For their

answers to that question men summoned both
their awareness of their present circumstances and
their anticipation of future prospects. David
Hawke has shown that the shopkeepers and ar-
tisans represented in the newly elected revolutionary committee in Philadelphia in the spring of
1776 were young businessmen "on their way up,"
and nearly all of them favored independence because they were motivated by economic pressures
and "their view of the future."[20] John M. Head
asserts that in New England and Virginia, in the
decade prior to 1774, "economic development . . .
constricted or declined," creating an ". . . atmosphere that made independence seem a
reasonable, safe course." But, in colonies like New
York, New Jersey, Pennsylvania, Delaware,
Maryland and South Carolina, in the same decade,
"economic development advanced at a steady or
rapid pace" and those provinces "sent delegates to
Congress who remained comparatively hesitant
about or who strongly opposed separation."[21]

Both those who argued for and those who
argued against a declaration of independence were
concerned about a potential disintegration of
social institutions, but they were not agreed in
their assessment of the effect that such a declaration would produce. Those opposing separation
claimed that the natural, inevitable accom-

paniment of independence would be a rending of
the social fabric and quick, deadly deterioration of
institutional and moral restraints. Men would
follow base instincts, lusting after easy gains in
time of rapid change. The men who championed
independence, on the other hand, argued that a
vacuum was already dangerously building as
regularly constituted governments vanished. The
disintegration of social controls, they asserted,
would proceed rapidly unless independence was
quickly declared and new governments structured
to reinstitute "law and order."

And, finally, what of the future? With independence, if successfully pursued, would come the
end of monarchical government in the United
Colonies and in its place would be erected experi-
ments in republican government. Unable to accept
such a future prospect, for philosophical or partisan reasons, some men fought the idea of independence as long as such a fight was possible and,
ultimately, withdrew their support from the
"cause." Others did not fear the prospect and
some eagerly embraced it. Actually, as time well
demonstrated, men could and did agree on the
assumption that a federation of republican
societies would be created on the continent, and
looked upon that creation as desirable, and yet
differed with each other greatly for republicanism

meant different things to different men. Thomas
Jefferson's vision of republican America was not
the same vision as that which stirred John Adams,
and Thomas Paine had still another vision.[22]
Omens of these differences were visible before
July, 1776, but in the critical months preceding
the act of separation it was possible for the men
who looked forward to independence and republican society to defer their personal differences
while confronting their opponents who rejected
the validity of the idea of independence.

That idea of independence was an extraordi-
narily complex idea, considered in unusually complex times. The questions posed above probably
represent only a portion of the determining questions that combined to lead some men toward an
affirmative response to the question of separation
and others to a negative reply. Herbert Friedenwald, in his book, focused his study of the politics
of independence upon only a few of the questions
listed, most notably the concern over republican
rule and internal politics. The fact that there were
unusually potent forces appears to be substantially
exhibited in the remaining records of the time.
They were not all that was combined to produce
the events, but they were an important part of the
idea of independence. A recent verdict pronounces
Friedenwald the " . . . most detailed, accurate,

and substantive" of all historians who have written about the politics of independence.[23] Certainly
his book is useful to later-day historians who, like
Friedenwald, would attempt to view the Declaration of Independence "from the standpoint of
the men who had a share in the events;" to those
who would try to understand the "attitude of
mind, to penetrate the well-springs" of the motives of the men who created this independent, republican federal nation.

FOOTNOTES

[1] Friedenwald, Herbert, *The Declaration of Independence*, (New York: The Macmillan Co., 1904), p. 172.

[2] Ibid, p. 172.

[3] The most extended biographical sketch of Friedenwald's life is Harry Schneiderman, "Herbert Friedenwald: Editor of the Jewish Year Book 1908–1912," *The American Jewish Year Book 5705* (Philadelphia, 1945), XLVI, 47–54. See also entries in *Who's Who in America,* volumes for 1899–1900 to 1945–46; obituary in *American Historical Review* (July, 1944), XLIX, 825. The Friedenwald family is described in Alexandra Lee Levin, *Vision: A Biography of Harry Friedenwald* (Philadelphia, 1964). Friedenwald's dissertation unfortunately has not been located at the University of Pennsylvania but is listed in *Doctors of Philosophy of the University of Pennsylvania Graduate School 1889–1927* (Philadelphia, 1927). I am indebted to Miss Sandra Page for help in gathering details about Friedenwald's life.

[4] See, as examples, "The Continental Congress," American Historical Association *Annual Report for 1894* (Washington, 1895), 227–236; *A Calendar of Washington Manuscripts in the Library of Congress* (Washington, 1901); "The Declaration of Independence," *International Monthly* (July, 1901), IV, 102–121.

[5] Between the two parts the reader will encounter Chapter VI, "Adopting and Signing of the Declaration." Much of this chapter is devoted to a discussion of whether or not the actual signing of the Declaration took place on July 4—a discussion concluding that it did *not*. Most historians writing since Friedenwald accept that conclusion, but Julian P. Boyd, in an analysis of the question, concludes that " . . . on the basis of evidence thus far advanced—all of it negative and some of it demonstrably untenable—the question cannot be regarded as closed." See *The Papers of Thomas Jefferson*, ed. Julian P. Boyd, 17 vols. (Princeton, 1950–date), I, 308.

[6] Carl Becker, *The Declaration of Independence: A Study in the History of Political Ideas* (New York, 1922), 226.

[7] Philip F. Detweiler, "The Changing Reputation of the Declaration of Independence: The First Fifty Years," *William and Mary Quarterly,* 3rd ser. (October, 1962), XIX, 558.

[8] Tyler's essay appeared in *North American Review* (July, 1896), CLXIII, 1–16; *The Literary History of the American Revolution* was published New York, 1897.

[9] Two years after Friedenwald's book appeared, John H. Hazelton would publish his exhaustive compendium, *The Declaration of Independence: Its History* (New York, 1906). Although almost devoid of interpretation, it is still a useful reference for detailed information about the Declaration.

[10] Friedenwald, p. vii.

[11] Compare, for example, Friedenwald's simplistic, undifferentiated descriptions with the detailing of divisions and factions in Merrill Jensen, *The Founding of a Nation: A History of the American Revolution, 1763–1776* (New York, 1968).

[12] Friedenwald, p. 18.

[13] Ibid., p. 32.

[14] Ibid., p. 79.

[15] Charles H. Lincoln, *The Revolutionary Movement in Pennsylvania 1760–1776* (Philadelphia, 1901); Carl Becker's essay "Growth of Revolutionary Parties and Methods in New York Province, 1765–1774," *American Historical Review* (October, 1901), VII, 56–76, anticipated his *History of Political Parties in the Province of New York* which would not appear until five years after Friedenwald's book was published.

[16] Friedenwald, p. 80.

[17] John M. Head, *A Time to Rend: An Essay on the Decision for American Independence* (Madison, 1968). A second recent treatment is David Hawke, *A Transaction of Free Men: The Birth and Course of the Declaration of Independence* (New York, 1964).

[18] Head, *A Time to Rend,* xv.

[19] John Alden, *A History of the American Revolution* (New York, 1969), 177.

[20] David Hawke, *In the Midst of Revolution* (Philadelphia, 1961), 100–101.

[21] Head, *A Time to Rend,* xiii, xiv.

[22] Staughton Lynd's *Intellectual Origins of American Radicalism* (New York, 1968), especially pp. 3–63, demonstrate how varied republican views actually were.

[23] Head, *A Time to Rend,* 187.

THE DECLARATION OF INDEPENDENCE
A BRIEF BIBLIOGRAPHY

Becker, Carl L. *The Declaration of Independence: A Study in the History of Political Ideas.* New York, 1922.

Boyd, Julian, P. *The Declaration of Independence: The Evolution of the Text as Shown in Facsimiles of Various Drafts by its Author, Thomas Jefferson.* Princeton, 1945.

————, ed. *The Papers of Thomas Jefferson.* Volume I. Princeton, 1950.

Detweiler, Philip F. "The Changing Reputation of the Declaration of Independence: The First Fifty Years," *William and Mary Quarterly,* 3rd series (October, 1962), XIX, 557–574.

Dumbauld, Edward. *The Declaration of Independence and What It Means Today.* Norman, Okla., 1950.

Ginsberg, Robert, ed. *A Casebook on the Declaration of Independence.* New York, 1967.

Hawke, David. *A Transaction of Free Men: The Birth and Course of the Declaration of Independence.* New York, 1964.

Hazelton, John M. *The Declaration of Independence: Its History.* New York, 1906.

XXXII

Head, John M. *A Time to Rend: An Essay on the Decision for American Independence.* Madison, Wis., 1968.

Howell, Wilbur Samuel. "The Declaration of Independence and Eighteenth-Century Logic," *William and Mary. Quarterly,* 3rd series (October, 1961), XVIII, 463–484.

Malone, Dumas. *The Story of the Declaration of Independence.* New York, 1954.

Tyler, Moses Coit. *The Literary History of the American Revolution, 1763–1783.* New York, 1897. I, 498–521.

CHRONOLOGY

1774

5 September–
26 October:

First Continental Congress at Philadelphia

1775

19 April:

Battle of Lexington and Concord

10 May:

Second Continental Congress meets at Philadelphia

14, 15 June:

Congress adopts New England army; chooses Washington commander-in-chief

6, 7 July:

Congress issues "Declaration of Causes and Necessity for Taking up Arms" and "Olive Branch" petition to the King

22 December:

the Prohibitory Act becomes law

1776

10 January:

Thomas Paine publishes *Common Sense*

13 February:

Congress tables address denying independence as objective

1 March:	Congress appoints Silas Deane foreign agent
23 March:	Congress authorizes American privateers
6 April:	Congress opens ports to other countries
13 April:	North Carolina empowers delegates to vote for independence
15 May:	Congress invites states to form "republican" governments; Virginia instructs delegates to move for independence
7 June:	Richard Henry Lee moves resolution in Congress for independence, alliances and confederation
1, 2 July:	Congress debates and approves Lee's resolution
4 July:	Congress approves the Declaration of Independence

THE

DECLARATION OF INDEPENDENCE

AN INTERPRETATION
AND AN ANALYSIS

The · M · Co ·

THE DECLARATION
OF INDEPENDENCE

AN INTERPRETATION
AND AN ANALYSIS

BY

HERBERT FRIEDENWALD, Ph.D.

New York

THE MACMILLAN COMPANY

LONDON: MACMILLAN & CO., Ltd.

1904

PRESS OF
THE NEW ERA PRINTING COMPANY
LANCASTER, PA.

TO MY MOTHER

PREFACE

It has been my endeavor to show, in the first five chapters, the close interrelation between the development of the authority and jurisdiction of the Continental Congress and the evolution of the sentiment for independence. The gradual, though occasionally rapid manner in which the Congress acquired power, and the ways in which this was exercised, went side by side with the growth of the idea that independence was a necessary outcome of the controversy between England and America, that had been raging for nearly fifteen years. As the authority and jurisdiction of the Congress were extended, it adopted various means to further the desire for independence. Also, as this desire became more widely spread, the Congress, the embodiment of the union sentiment, acting for all and in behalf of all, gained additional strength. The highest point of its power was reached on July 4, 1776. It was never again so powerful as on the day it declared independence of England. The decline of its authority dates from this time, when the first steps were taken to define the limits to its jurisdiction, by means of the Articles of Confederation. The states then began to acquire power at the cost of the Congress, ultimately culmi-

nating in its complete overthrow and the establishment of a new federal government under the Constitution.

In order to describe the beginnings of the Congress and of independence it has not been thought
necessary to go over again the oft-told, though as yet
inadequately told story of the rise of the American
revolutionary movement. A familiarity with the
main facts of that history is assumed. Only such
of the earlier phases of the controversy, as bear immediately upon independence, have been touched
upon in the opening chapter. In one sense Chalmers
was correct in dating independence from the first
days of the settlement of the colonies. In another,
the events preceding the Congress of 1774, are to be
differentiated from those happening after that date,
when ideas of establishing independence first had
their rise. There is no evidence of a conscious striving for independence in the earlier period; there is
none even previous to November, 1775, but after
that date it appears on every hand with a force that
rendered the final outcome inevitable.

In the explanation of the meaning of the various
clauses of the Declaration, embodied in chapters X
and XI, I have not attempted to deal with every example of a colonial grievance that might with propriety be assumed to have been held in mind by the
framers of that document. Only the grievances of

particular significance, and those that had attained greatest prominence are referred to. The limit (1763) fixed by the Congress of 1774 as the starting point of the controversy, has been adhered to in the main; not, however, because it is any part of my intention to hold that the causes of the revolution had their origin at so late a period, but for the reason that the principal grievances complained of reached their most aggravating development after that date.

The earlier chapters are in some respects a preliminary study, in part an abstract of a larger, more detailed work on this subject for which I have been collecting material for some years. The first incentive to undertake it was received under the guidance of Professor John Bach McMaster, to whom is owing a debt which it is a pleasure to acknowledge here. He has put me under additional obligation by his kindness in reviewing a portion of the manuscript, and for encouragement given me to push the work to completion.

For helpful criticism of some of the manuscript and all of the proofs, I am indebted to Prof. John L. Stewart. And I have to thank my kind friends, Miss Henrietta Szold, Mr. Joseph Jacobs, Dr. Cyrus Adler, and Mr. C. L. Sulzberger, for reading the proofs and for many valuable suggestions.

For purposes of convenience I have throughout cited Peter Force's well-known *American Archives* as *Force*. The references to *Jefferson's Writings* are to Ford's edition, and those to *Mass. State Papers* to Bradford's *Speeches of the Governors of Massachusetts, from 1765 to 1775; and the Answers of the House of Representatives to the same,* etc., Boston, 1818.

TABLE OF CONTENTS

xi

CHAPTER IX

CHAPTER X

CHAPTER XI

APPENDIX

THE

DECLARATION OF INDEPENDENCE

AN INTERPRETATION AND AN ANALYSIS

CHAPTER I

The Popular Uprising

During the period of more than one hundred years preceding the Declaration of Independence, repeated occasion offered for differences of opinion to arise between the crown and the colonies, over questions of policy and the interpretation of constitutional law. Beginning in controversy over governmental methods, earnest discussion led on to serious dispute that finally culminated in engendering much bitterness of feeling. Owing, however, to the lack of a definite British colonial policy consistently carried out, or, more exactly, the failure to carry out consistently the existing policy, the colonies were in large measure allowed to grow up neglected. When laws were passed by Parliament designed, in pursuance of the mercantile theories of the age, to control the commerce and productions of the

colonies, for the benefit of England, they were
either not enforced at all, or enforced with such laxity, as practically to nullify their intended purpose.[1]
This neglect had a double effect: it deprived the
home country of the commercial rewards that would
have been hers had these acts been enforced rigidly,
and it allowed the colonists to develop their commerce largely on the lines suggested by an intelligent
perception of the natural advantages of their geographical relation to the West Indies. In like manner, the control of their political affairs by the crown
was exercised with such leniency, in the main, as
ultimately to produce a condition that has been admirably described as " virtual independence with relations of mutual good-will."[2]

Upon the accession of Grenville to power in 1763,
the attempt was made to accomplish the impossible
task of subverting peacefully the multiform customs
and precedents that a century of license had permitted to be established. If at this time King, ministry and Parliament could have fashioned a statesman in whose mind would be found a combination
of the wisdom of a Moses and a Solomon, with the
philosophy of a Plato and an Aristotle, he might
have carried through to success the policy which

[1] The number of British acts of Parliament affecting the
commerce and industry of the colonies in force at this time,
footed up a total of thirty.

[2] C. F. Adams, *Life and Works of John Adams,* I, 133.

Grenville undertook to initiate. But nothing short of some such superhuman aggregate of mental resources could have accomplished it. On the other hand, it would appear as if Grenville and his successors endeavored to carry out their plans in a manner pre-designed to create as much irritation as the circumstances would allow. If, instead, the British authorities had, in dealing with the colonies, exercised some of the tactful diplomacy which has won so many triumphs in the larger field of international affairs, the separation might have been postponed for a considerable term of years.[1]

Further, a serious tactical blunder was made, by yielding to the clamor of the colonies against the Stamp Act, by reason of which it was repealed on March 17, 1766. At the same time the act since generally known as the Declaratory Act was made into law.[2] It was unwise to pass laws and then allow them to be annulled by non-enforcement. It was in the highest degree injudicious to enact a measure containing many of the provisions of the Stamp Act. But the crowning act of folly came with the repeal of an obnoxious act upon the occasion of the first show of resistance to it, by means of the revolutionary memorials of the Stamp Act Congress of 1765. Had the Grenville ministry or its successor, the

[1] This was Franklin's view.
[2] See Chapter XI.

Rockingham Whigs,[1] determined at all hazards to
enforce the law with a high hand, for this purpose
calling in the military arm of the government, there
would have been an end to resistance, and the revolution would have been postponed for many years.
When troops were finally sent over they availed little,
for they were few in number, were utilized in no
spirited manner, and served only to raise the issue of
quartering troops without consent, in time of peace,
causing the additional irritation which culminated
in the clash at Boston on March 5, 1770. But in the
beginning a large force would have had a decided
effect. For no sort of extra-legal, intercolonial political organizations existed as yet, nor any sufficient feeling of the necessity for united action, such
as grew up during the first ten years of the controversy. At the end of that time the ramifications
of the newly created committees of correspondence
and the like, were so widely extended as to touch
the popular mind at every point. This is evidenced

[1] The fact that the Rockingham Whigs were of a different
political complexion from the Grenville ministry, and consequently had no interest in enforcing the unwelcome acts of
its predecessors, does not affect the case. For they immediately proceeded to pass the Declaratory Act, which (though
little attention was paid to it at the time by the colonists)
ultimately proved more serious in its consequences than was
anticipated, when an attempt was made to live up to its provisions. The colonists at first regarded it as but another
British act passed with no intention of being enforced.

by the fact that only nine colonies were represented at the Stamp Act Congress, all but three of the delegations having been elected by the respective legal assemblies. Ten years later, when but one colony failed to respond,[1] only five of the delegations to the Congress of 1774 were elected by the assemblies. The revolutionary organization was by this time so complete that it mattered little whether or not assemblies were in session; delegates were elected none the less in a regular and orderly manner throughout the colonies.[2]

If anything approaching an adequate conception respecting the temper and attitude of mind of the colonies existed in England, it was not shown in any of the legislation enacted, beginning with the passage of the Townshend Acts of 1767;[3] nor is there any evidence of the existence of an appreciation of the extraordinary ability for dialectics that had developed in the minds of the foremost Americans. Moreover, through the Stamp Act Congress, by its successful resistance to the Stamp Act, the colonists had their first taste of the efficiency of united action against Great Britain, when the interests of all were thought to be at stake. It had

[1] Georgia.

[2] New Hampshire, Virginia, North Carolina, and Georgia were not represented at the Stamp Act Congress because their respective assemblies were not in session and there was no other organization to supply the deficiency.

[3] See Chapter XI.

been the custom for a colony to appeal by petition to the King when any grievance weighed too heavily upon it, and often with success. It was natural, therefore, that they should appeal in common when all were concerned alike.

But by adopting memorials to Lords and Commons, at the Stamp Act Congress, at the same time as a petition to the King was formulated, they went further than they had any idea of going, and took the first step on the road to independence. For this marks the beginning of an entire change in the character of the controversy. Hitherto dispute had always been with the crown. But Parliament, by the Sugar Act[1] and the Stamp Act, had projected itself into American affairs, by passing laws having the purpose of raising revenue by direct taxation, and the colonists were not slow to make that branch of the British government a party to their disputes. This, however, is the only occasion on which the colonists as a body addressed Parliament directly, and demonstrates the unformed character of the colonial opposition. After opportunity had been given for an interchange of views respecting the grounds of the colonial contentions, and a definite stand had been taken, the tactical error of appealing to Parliament was not repeated. As the controversy advanced, though Parliament was held

[1] April 5, 1764. See Chapter XI.

at fault, the doctrine was consistently maintained
that the King had it within his power to right their
wrongs, and to him must all appeals be made. The
colonists gradually renounced all consideration of
parliamentary control, and they would stultify themselves by appealing for redress to a power whose
authority they would not recognize.

Further, an examination of the declaration of
rights and of the petition and memorials of the
Stamp Act Congress discloses a fundamental difference between them and the documents issued
subsequently. The theory of the natural right of
Englishmen to enjoy the blessings of the British
constitution, to representation, to taxation only by
representatives, and to trial by jury, figure con-
spicuously, it is true, in the state papers of the
Stamp Act Congress. But, side by side with these,
and raised to equal importance, were put the economic reasons why the enforcement of the Stamp
Act and the recently revised trade laws would prove
burdensome. The colonies would be drained of
specie, they held, rendering it impossible to pay the
debts due England's merchants; the profits Great
Britain would derive from her trade with the colonies would be decreased materially, because they
would be made so poor as to be unable to purchase needed commodities; and they would, therefore, be unable to bear the burden of paying 'the

taxes imposed by the Stamp Act, short of absolute
ruin.   Another point should be noted: the tone
of these appeals is far more moderate.   Rights are
asserted with much less vehemence, and there is
much more show of a conciliatory spirit than is evident in any of the documents produced by the next
congress.[1]

But a new phase was entered upon with the repeal
of the Stamp Act and the passage of the Declaratory
Act.   In this the assertion of the colonists that
their own assemblies had the sole and exclusive right
of imposing duties and taxes was denounced, and
it was specifically declared that the colonies " have
been, are, and of right ought to be, subordinate
unto, and dependent upon the imperial crown of
Great Britain; and that the King's majesty, by and
with the advice and consent of the lords spiritual
and temporal, and commons of Great Britain, in
parliament assembled, had, hath, and of right ought
to have, full power and authority to make laws and
statutes of sufficient force and validity to bind the
colonies and people of America, subjects of the
crown of Great Britain, in all cases whatsoever."[2]
The economic burdens of which the colonies com-

[1] The proceedings of the Stamp Act Congress are to be
found in Niles' *Principles and Acts of the Revolution*, 1822,
451 *et seq.*

[2] The text of the act can be found most conveniently in
MacDonald's *Select Charters Illustrative of American History,*
1606–1775, 316.

plained having been removed, they were led to hope that since the change in the ministry, and the return to power of the Whigs, Rockingham would not enforce the revised trade regulations. Their economic grievances being practically at an end, the Declaratory Act, another of Great Britain's measures of unwisdom, was made the means of carrying on the controversy, whose entire character was now transformed from one in which economic and political elements played an equal part to one having almost exclusively a political basis. Complaint respecting the effects and workings of any of the subsequent British acts, is never again based on grounds that may be regarded as primarily economic. The only economic phase of the subsequent controversy is found when non-importation agreements are entered into, with the view to oppressing British merchants engaged in colonial commerce to such an extent as to induce them to espouse the cause of the colonists, and make them work to have the obnoxious acts repealed to save themselves from ruin.

The repressive measures of Hillsborough of 1768, and the retention of the duty on tea in April, 1770, when the other Townshend taxes of 1767[1] were repealed, are of a piece with the Declaratory Act in their effect in emphasizing the transformation of the

[1] The nature and effect of these several acts are described in chapters X and XI.

character of the dispute. The tea duty was retained for the same reason that prompted the passage of the Declaratory Act—to maintain the principle of parliamentary authority—and was but another in the long list of deeds of unwisdom of the
British government. By repealing the other duties
Parliament yielded to popular clamor, as in the repeal
of the Stamp Act, but retained an obnoxious measure
that was to prove a fruitful source of further irritation. A partial repeal, with the retention of one
duty designed for a purpose only too well known in
America, was folly worse confounded, and showed
that there was no real conception in England of the
earnestness and determination of the Americans, nor
of the nature of the independent development of
political institutions produced by a century of experience. The events that had transpired in the five
years succeeding the passage of the Stamp Act were
productive of great results, so that by 1770 the controversy had been pushed to the point from which
must issue either complete submission of the colonies
to England, or else independence.

In Great Britain at the end of the hundred years
subsequent to the Puritan Revolution, the reaction
had reproduced a virtual kingly autocracy, though
within certain legal and constitutional bounds. By
force of his dominating personality, the King,
though nominally guided by his ministers, had made

himself the directing head of the nation's affairs, and practically controlled his cabinet and Parliament as he saw fit. In America, where the structure of society was far simpler, there had been no such reaction. On the contrary, there had been a constant development along the democratic lines made familiar by the popular uprisings under Cromwell. In consequence the political ideas of Locke passed current not alone in the Puritan colonies of New England, but were received at their face value in the other colonies which at their foundation had nothing in common with the Puritan ideals. By reason of the extent to which the colonists participated in their political affairs throughout the colonies, the laxity with which parliamentary enactments were enforced, and the leniency shown by the crown, a complete administrative machinery of their own was developed in many respects far in advance of anything of a similar nature existing in Great Britain.. In other words they had brought over with them a perfect familiarity with British constitutional and administrative forms, which, owing to the more democratic nature of the conditions under which they lived, produced a body politic in which practically every property owner had a stake. Out of this was evolved an attachment for their own methods, as strong as that of any parent for its child.

The questions at issue previous to 1763 had been

argued with the crown, either directly or through
the royal governors, often with great earnestness,
though only on occasion with a show of heat. But
with the change in the nature of the dispute from
one between King and colonies, in which the points
of disagreement were localised, were peculiar to
each colony, and did not permit of any united opposition, to one between Parliament and colonies,
in which, among others, the principle of taxation was
at issue, affecting all alike, the natural passions
were aroused that are ordinarily engendered when
the attempt is made by an outsider to appropriate and convert to his own use what one believes
to be his own property, the fruit of his toil. Their
point of view was admirably stated by Burke when
he said " a great people who have their property,
without any reserve, disposed of by another people
at an immense distance from them, will not think
themselves in the enjoyment of liberty."[1] That taxation without representation was tyranny, and nothing
less, became the doctrine universally held. It was repeatedly reiterated that, by the nature of their location, they had and could have representation only in
their assemblies, by which alone they would therefore
consent to be taxed.[2] As one man they flung back

[1] Speech on " State of the Nation," *Works* II, 170.
[2] It is true that Otis in his pamphlet *The Rights of the
British Colonies Asserted,* 1764, advocated colonial representation in Parliament, but this idea did not attain to gen-

and would have none of the British idea of virtual
representation, which was that the colonies were not
less represented than the people of Great Britain,
five-sixths of whom had no share in the election of
members of Parliament, by reason of the corrupt
and inefficient British system. That a member of
Parliament was as much a member for the whole
empire as for the constituency which sent him, was
the theory held as largely then as now. But it did
not appeal to the colonists, grown accustomed to the
benefits of actual representation.

The unanimity of the acceptance of the idea
of the interrelation of representation and taxation,
as also the wide extent of the belief in the theories
that man was born with certain natural, inalienable
rights, and that government derived its origin from
a compact for mutual protection, was due to the remarkable series of disquisitions on the rights of the
colonies, the nature and extent of these rights, and
the constitutional limitations to parliamentary control, which the five years of discussion had produced.
Every man who was ready with the pen,—and the
number of these indicated an unusual diffusion of
skill in political debate,—contributed his share,
though the productions of men like James Otis,

eral adoption. In the Declaration of Rights of 1774 it was
specifically stated as the colonial contention that the colonies
could be represented only in the colonial legislatures. See
Declaration of Rights, article 4.

Samuel and John Adams, Richard Bland, Daniel Dulany, John Dickinson, and Stephen Hopkins, stand out in especial prominence.   Without going into an examination of the merits of their arguments, it suffices to draw attention to the fact that they served to familiarize the public, in the widest possible degree, with a reasonable theory of the origins of government, and of the constitutional relations between the colonies and Great Britain.   They made every freeholder believe and maintain that he possessed certain rights and privileges which were far too sacred to permit of being infringed by any acts of King or Parliament, and for which it was his duty to contend, with all the power that in him lay.   The men who wrote these often stirring pamphlets were the same who in legislative assemblies embodied their thoughts in the form of resolutions and memorials, and thus gave them not only the widest circulation, but a semi-legal character as well, making them the acts of the people.   There were able counterblasts, too, notably from the well-attuned trumpet of Jonathan Boucher, proclaimer of the sacred rights of kings and government.   But they were not sufficiently harmonious in these preliminary stages to make any strong impression.   Not until the later point was reached of the practical denial of parliamentary authority, dating from 1774, does this opposition become in any way important.

In fact, one of the most striking elements in the
preliminary stages of the revolution, is the extraordinary unanimity of opinion as to the existence
of rights and of serious infringements of them prevailing throughout the colonies.

Not much more was required, therefore, to make
the parties at issue fall farther and farther apart.
Nor was there a question as to whether the colonies
or the home government had the greater weight of
authoritative legal opinion on its side.   It has come
to be admitted that the preponderance of constitutional law was with those favoring the parliamentary contention, and that both English political
parties were at one in their belief in the legality
of parliamentary dominance over the colonies as embodied in the Declaratory Act, whatever may have
been their differences on other points.   No one had
firmer faith in this doctrine than Pitt himself, the
idol of America, under whose ministry the Act was
passed.   The extent of administrative development
in America through the legislative assemblies, and
the firmness of the faith that full justification for
the colonists' attitude was found in the current interpretation of the origin and ends of government,
should not have been overlooked by the British
statesmen.   That there was a power above the constitution from which rights were derived, was an
idea as generally diffused as that Americans were

free-born English subjects and entitled to all their
rights and privileges.   In contests over the interpretation of constitutional and political theories, the
question is ultimately decided not by the weight of
legal precedents, but by the sacrifices which the parties at issue are willing to make when points of
difference prove irreconcilable.   In fundamentals,
as has been well said, all constitutional questions are
"questions of power, and not of law."[1]   The
theories of America and England were so much at
variance by this time that nothing short of absolute submission of the one or the other could bring
about a peaceful solution.   That the latter was not
to result, the events of the four years succeeding
1770 made inevitable.   Clashes between soldiery
and populace were succeeded by repeated acts of
violence in resistance to authority in which the
military arm played little or no part.   A spirit of
lawlessness, so far as the enforcement of British
acts was concerned, was manifested side by side
with the most perfect respect for legislative acts of
the colonists' own creation.

In the meantime, as assemblies were being prorogued throughout the colonies, and as this administrative machinery was in danger of breaking down,
recourse was had to a new expedient for political
control, the Committees of Correspondence.   At first

[1] Sir James Fitzjames Stephen, *Horæ Sabbaticæ*, III, 120.

appointed by the assemblies, they gradually came into existence almost everywhere by original authority of the people, and their variety of forms made necessary by difference of conditions, is a striking witness to the wide diffusion of, familiarity with, and capacity for political organization.[1] They served to keep the colonists in touch with each other, by extending their activities even beyond the bounds of the individual colonies. They thus performed the function of an intercolonial clearing house, through which the inhabitants of one colony were made familiar with the occurrences taking place in another. When, therefore, Great Britain in 1774 began her policy of attempting to coerce the colonies into submission, it was too late to meet with success, for an effective instrument for resistance had been developed as the result of the previous ten years of discussion. Moreover, as was ultimately proved, the colonists were willing to sacrifice their all for the maintenance of the principles which they firmly believed were involved. Familiarity with the uses to which their extra-legal committee organizations could be put, for purposes of colonial and intercolonial communication, made it natural that still greater reliance should be placed upon them when the question of convening a continental con-

[1] On Committees of Correspondence and their significance, see the able treatment which they receive at the hand of Dr. Edward D. Collins, in *Rep't American Hist. Assn.*, 1901, I, 243.

gress for mutual support was before them. Thus
it happened, that of the twelve colonies sending
delegates to the Congress but five acted through
their assemblies, though three[1] of these were so
completely in control of the revolutionists as scarcely
to be of significance in this connection. All of the
remaining delegations were chosen by some form
of committee organization.

The Congress which convened at Carpenter's Hall
in Philadelphia, on September 5, 1774, had, therefore, a much more popular basis than any Congress
heretofore called together. And whereas recourse
was had in the past to the various committees of
correspondence for purposes of united action, under
the more difficult and complex conditions that had
arisen, their place was now to be taken by this new
engine of political organization. The Congress and
the local committees bore to each other relations of
interdependence: the committees created the Congress, and the Congress in turn looked to the committees to enforce its recommendations. The voice
that the committees had in calling the Congress into
being, thereby giving it a popular character, spoke
out even to the extent of outlining the work that it
was to undertake.

In their instructions, either to delegates directly,
or to committees that were to have a share in the

[1] Rhode Island, Connecticut, and Massachusetts.

election of delegates, the people gave expression to their desires in not uncertain tones. The credentials which the delegates bore to this first Continental Congress were in the main of the same character. They were authorized in general to devise measures that would extricate the colonies from the difficulties with which they were beset, to state the rights and privileges to which on constitutional grounds they were entitled, and to endeavor to restore harmony, mutual confidence, and union.[1] Behind these credentials, however, and of a much more specific character, were the instructions issued to the delegates by their constituent bodies. Three days after the Boston Port Bill reached that town her citizens gave expression to their view that the salvation of North America depended on the other colonies coming to a general agreement to stop all importation.[2] It was on this hint that the colonies spoke for a general Congress. At the same time, the suggestion of obtaining redress by the adoption of commercial restrictions was taken up by no less than six of the colonies. Definitive resolutions were passed in Maryland,[3] Pennsylvania, New Jersey, Delaware, Vir-

[1] The credentials are to be found in *Journal of Congress* for 1774.

[2] May 13, 1774, *Force,* 4th, I, 331.

[3] Maryland's resolutions were passed June 22, 1774, *Force,* 4th, I, 439; Pennsylvania's on July 15, *ibid.,* 555; New Jersey's July 21, *ibid.,* 624; Delaware's August 2, *ibid.,* 668; Virginia's

ginia, and North Carolina, authorizing their representatives to enter into non-importation and non-exportation agreements if the representatives of the other colonies were of the same mind. South Carolina alone had considered the matter and voted it down, substituting general instructions, and proved later on the stumbling block over which the Congress came near falling.[1] Maryland and Virginia went even further and embodied their views respecting commercial aggression, in the credentials to their delegates, while New Jersey and Delaware pledged themselves in advance to support the Congress in whatever action it might take in addition to these measures.

Thus the Congress before it met was committed to issuing a statement of the rights and grievances of the colonists and to the adoption of the only powerful and efficient means at hand to effect the repeal of the obnoxious acts—a non-importation and non-exportation agreement. It was generally appreciated that their objects could not be attained without some form of central organization which should extend beyond any hitherto known. The Congress, therefore, was the natural advance from

August 1–6, *ibid.*, 689; North Carolina's August 27, *ibid.*, 689. In Rhode Island especially, the town meetings expressed similar views, as was the case in many instances elsewhere.

[1] See John Adams' Diary, *Works*, II, 382 *et seq.*, 393 *et seq.*; McCrady, *South Carolina under Royal Gov't.*, 762 *et seq.*

the committee organizations, and served as the expression of the popular desire for united action and for the creation of a policy on which such action might be based.

The Congress in turn showed its appreciation of the fact that it was the creature of the popular will and dependent on it for the success of its resolves by three acts of striking significance. The first was the unanimous and immediate endorsement of the resolutions of the Suffolk County Committee, recommending " a perseverance in the same firm and temperate conduct as expressed in the resolutions."[1] Firm they undoubtedly were, but a perusal will disclose that " temperate " is scarcely the other adjective by which they should, in truth, be described.[2] The pledge of Suffolk County, to support whatever the Congress determined on, went a long way toward influencing it in taking this radical action. Their assurance was the first information of this nature officially conveyed, as the resolutions of the Congress thereon were the first public expression of the fact that the colonies would support each other and stand as one man in the contest. By the endorsement of these resolutions the Congress gave the sanction of its authority to the most recent American view respecting the constitu-

[1] *Journal of Congress*, September 17, 1774.

[2] The Suffolk Resolutions are to be found in the *Journal of Congress*, September 17, 1774.

tional relations of Parliament and the colonies, that of no legislation without representation. From this to war for independence was inevitably but a short step.

Secondly, came the letter to General Gage[1] demanding the cessation of activity on the part of his troops, in which the Congress proclaims that its members are "appointed the guardians" of the rights and liberties of the colonies. And, lastly, we have the clauses of the Articles of Association, (practically an ordinance of nullification, and the expression of the previously announced popular desire), by which enforcement of its provisions was to be ensured, and which mark a still further development in government by committee. These Articles as finally adopted and signed on October 20, prohibited the importation of British products after December 1, 1774, as also of certain enumerated commodities from the West Indies, and of East India tea no matter whence derived; nor were any slaves to be brought in after that date nor the trade in them continued. No tea was to be used or purchased on which any duty had been paid, and none whatever after the first of March, 1775. After September 10, 1775, unless all the acts complained of had been repealed in the interval, no commodities, excepting " rice to Europe," were to

[1] October 11, 1774.

be exported to Great Britain, Ireland, or the West Indies. Committees were to be chosen in every county, city, and town, by those qualified to vote for representatives in the legislature. Their business was to see that the Association was not violated, and that violators of it should be practically boycotted. The Committees of Correspondence, further, were given plenary instructions to examine entries at the custom houses to obtain evidence of the violation of the Association. In addition to the Articles of Association, this Congress adopted a Declaration of Rights, a petition to the King, and issued addresses to the people of Great Britain, to the inhabitants of the colonies, and a special one to those of Quebec.

Among the very earliest of the important acts of the first Congress was the decision, reached only after much discussion, to limit any statement of rights to such " as have been infringed by acts of the British parliament since the year 1763, postponing the further consideration of the general state of American rights to a future day."[1] This is self-explanatory and gave a definitiveness to the controversy that would not otherwise have been obtained.

To frame a declaration of rights was one of the principal duties of this Congress, thereby to fix a common ground upon which all could stand. But

[1] *Journal of Congress,* September 24; John Adams, *Works,* I, 160; II, 370 *et seq.*

at the outset a stumbling block was met with, when consideration was given to the extent to which the authority of Parliament was to be recognized in this declaration. Upon this point there was wide divergence of opinion, and various propositions were advanced. Some proposed drawing the distinction between internal and external taxation, some advocated the denial of the applicability to the colonies of any statute wherein taxation was intended, and some even the disavowal of any parliamentary authority whatever. Finally John Adams came forward with his equivocal compromise proposition. In this, while claiming the exclusive power to legislate in their own representative assemblies upon all matters of taxation and internal polity, subject only to the negative of their sovereign, the willingness was expressed, from the necessity of the case and for the purpose of " securing the commercial advantages of the whole empire to the mother country," to consent to the operation of all laws regulating commerce with other countries, " excluding every idea of taxation, internal or external, for raising a revenue on the subjects in America without their consent." [1] This forms the fourth of the rights embodied in this declaration, and with the sixth is the only one which did not meet with unanimous approval. The preamble of the Declaration of Rights,

[1] John Adams, *Works*, II, 397; *Journal of Congress*.

as passed on October 14, contains a summary of all the acts of Parliament passed " since the close of the last war " which are viewed as infringing rights, and enacted with a view to subjecting the colonists to a jurisdiction and control which they cannot recognize. Added to this their assemblies have been frequently dissolved, and their " dutiful, humble, loyal, and reasonable " petitions treated with contempt. In consequence, they, the duly appointed, elected, and constituted representatives of the colonies have come together " in order to obtain such establishment, as that their religion, laws and liberties may not be subverted." Following comes an enumeration of the rights and privileges to which, " by the immutable laws of nature, the principles of the English constitution, and the several charters and compacts," they are entitled. These are (1) the right to life, liberty and property ; (2) the rights, liberties and immunities of natural born Englishmen, (3) none of which was lost by emigration ; (4) representation in their own legislatures and taxation by them only ; (5) enjoyment of the benefits of the common law of England, trial by jury, and (6) the English statutes in existence at the time of colonization and applicable to their condition ; (7) the immunities and privileges granted in the charters and secured by the codes of provincial laws ; (8) the right to assemble, to consider grievances, and to petition; (9) that it is against law to keep a standing army in the colonies in time of peace; (10) and that it is destructive of the freedom of America for legislative power to be exercised by a council appointed to hold office during pleasure of the crown. An enumeration of the thirteen specific laws in which these rights and privileges are infringed follows, with the demand for their repeal if harmony is to be restored. Submission to them is declared out of the question, and to ensure their repeal an agreement for non-importation, non-consumption and non-exportation is to be entered into, and addresses to the people of Great Britain and America, as also a loyal petition to the King to be prepared.

The place of the address to Parliament of the Stamp Act Congress, was now taken by the address to the people of Great Britain, (the work of John Jay), and illustrates the point adverted to before respecting the development of the controversy. What aim it was hoped to further by this address is not quite clear, for the addressors were as familiar as we now are with the little influence the people at large had upon England's politics. But it was thought well to cherish the fiction that the people were responsible for the character of the Parliament they supposedly elected, as the assemblies represented the people of the colonies. And they were, therefore, appealed to in the hope " that the magnanimity and justice of the British nation will furnish a parliament of such wisdom, independence, and public spirit, as may save the violated rights of the whole empire, from the devices of wicked ministers and evil counsellors, whether in or out of office ; and thereby restore that harmony, friendship, and fraternal affection, between all the inhabitants of His Majesty's kingdoms and territories so ardently wished for, by every true and honest American."

The address to the people of the colonies, the handiwork of Richard Henry Lee, served as an explanation and justification of the proceedings of the Congress, and is a remarkably calm and well-written recital of rights and grievances and of the proposals for redress. The humble though firm petition to the King, bearing the impress of Dickinson's able mind, was an admirably conceived document, and might have impressed a more obstinate king had he been open to reason. The address to the people of Quebec was an attempt to draw them into the controversy, but had no better success than the more energetic measures of the spring of 1776.[1]

Naturally, the revolutionary measures that had been adopted met with the disapproval of large numbers of people, who now voiced their dissenting

[1] See pp. 83–84.

views in the public prints. They saw that if persisted in, civil war would be the end, and while
they were willing to follow the leaders to the verge
of the precipice, they stopped in horror at the sight
of the chaotic abyss beyond. An opposition party
now sprang into existence, destined to have a
serious influence upon the conduct of affairs within
as well as without the Congress.

Spirited and outspoken as were the resolutions of
the Congress of 1774 in stating their demands,
there is no sign among them all that can rightly be
interpreted as indicating a wish for the establishment, even remotely, of an independent government.
Nor could there have been. For the instructions
to the delegates, and their credentials as well, were
practically unanimous in expressing the desire that
such measures as were passed, should be not less in
the interest of the restoration of harmony and union
than for the redress of grievances.

It is questionable, also, whether such avowed
radicals as John and Samuel Adams, Jefferson, and
Patrick Henry, would have advocated independence
in earnest at this time, had the opportunity been
favorable. To speak loosely as they did, to the
effect that if matters did not take a turn for the
better, independence was the inevitable outcome, was
far different from establishing a definite concerted
plan having that aim in view. They were too

skilled as politicians to be the upholders of a policy that would have damned at the outset the cause into which they had thrown themselves body and soul. Many months had to pass, and many irritating events occur during the year following the adjournment of the Congress of 1774, before we find the tide changing, and the country drifting at first, and then guided skillfully, into the swift current of independence.[1]

Having performed the functions for which it was called into being, the Congress dissolved on October 26, to meet again, if occasion required, in May of the following year.

[1] See in this connection Sparks' *Washington*, II, Appendix X, and Winsor, *Narrative and Critical History*, VI, 248–251, 255.

CHAPTER II

THE CONGRESS FINDING ITSELF

Practically the same men who had separated
in October of the previous year, and representing the same politically organized bodies, found
themselves once more entrusted with the affairs of
America, when they reconvened at Philadelphia on
May 10, 1775. They had used the interval to good
purpose, and throughout the colonies had been instrumental in having the acts of the previous Congress supported by resolutions of assemblies, conventions, and committees. So that they were reassured,
if any reassurance were needed, that so far as they
had gone, they had properly given expression to the
desires of their electors. But they were now face
to face with new and far different problems. By
the accident of circumstance, the clash at arms at
Lexington and Concord, duties and reponsibilities
were thrust upon them that none had given thought
to a few months before. And in undertaking these
new activities, the Congress had no precedent to
guide it, nor any instructions even from its constituents to follow as before. It was, therefore, free
and untrammeled so long as it kept within the
bounds of popular support.

All the country was drifting about hopelessly, looking for some pilot to show the way. For now that the controversy had been pushed to the breaking point, real parties were forming. Many who were willing to follow so long as peaceful measures alone were resorted to, became hearty conservatives as soon as they saw civil war imminent. Others, seeing the consequences of the denial of parliamentary authority staring them in the face, had not made up their minds which side to join. These two groups formed probably a majority of the inhabitants, and in some districts of New York and Pennsylvania were greatly in preponderance. But their influence was weakened since they lacked not only an organization, but seemingly, even the power to organize,[1] though they were not backward in keeping their pens busy writing pamphlets and taking active part in the heated discussions in the gazettes. Consequently the well-organized revolutionary party, represented for America at large by the Congress, controlled affairs. The Congress, therefore, was compelled to assume the directing hand and provide the rule of conduct, the more so as the revolutionary organizations, in colony after colony, were looking to it for advice and direction, especially in all that concerned military affairs. This dependence on the Congress and the authority it derived there-

[1] See Van Tyne, *Loyalists in Am. Revolution*, 85, 87.

from, carried with them a gradual development of a spirit of subordination to its will, on the part of those controlling the revolutionary movement. The Congress thus grew, from an impotent body with vague powers designed at first to prepare petitions and addresses, into one having practically complete control of the affairs of a people engaged in a war of revolution, with all that such control implies. Though this evolution is the most important civil and political phenomenon of the period, it was a perfectly natural development, since the leading spirits and ablest men were in Philadelphia, and they saw to it that the new power assumed its authority with caution and wielded it with skill.

For the understanding of the events of the next year it is all-important that the growth of the power and authority of the Congress, the manner of their exercise, and the method of enforcing its decisions upon points of policy, be clearly held in mind. Actually the creature of the colonies, representing the united sentiment of them all, the Congress was much stronger than any one colony. It stood for union and was, therefore, compelled to pursue every measure looking to the tightening of the chains. By so doing and by frowning upon every individual action that might lead to disunion and consequent weakening of its own powers, it succeeded in ever strengthening itself. So that by the time it reached

its highest point of authority (July 4, 1776) we
have unfolded before us the phenomenon of a politically organized body, the creature of individual
political organizations, deriving all its strength and
sanction from them, dependent for its existence
upon their good will, yet with no limits to its authority other than those of the reason and good
sense of its members. Gradually it procured so
much power as to be able to dictate to the colonies
how to shape their own administrative organizations, and finally was able to advance to the extreme
point of declaring them independent of the government that had always controlled them. The successful manner in which this was consummated is
demonstrated by the support given to its acts
throughout the colonies. In all this the Congress
relied on and fostered the democratic elements of
which, in large measure, it was the revolutionary
outcome. Without so doing the revolution would
never have attained so much of success as it did
before outside aid was called upon. It suited the
purposes of those who fostered the revolution to
emphasize the natural rights to which they believed
themselves entitled. This very emphasis aroused
the minds of " the multitude," (as it was generally
termed) to a knowledge that they too had rights
which had been denied them hitherto,—that by the
restrictions upon the franchise, upon representation,

3

and by other means, they had been deprived of participation in the government. It required many years of agitation before they finally came into full possession of their own, but the beginnings were made now. The Congress saw plainly that if it was to rely on the democracy to fight its battles in the field, the democracy must be shown certain favors in return. Only the first moves had been made toward the creation of a continental army, when the Congress pronounced as its policy this reliance on the people for support. In its most definite form it was embodied in the advice given, in November and December, 1775, to the colonies of New Hampshire, South Carolina, and Virginia, respecting the creation of new forms of government. In each instance the Congress recommends the calling of " a full and free representation of the people,"[1] to establish the form of government by which they are to be controlled. This is far different in character from the earlier advice given to Massachusetts,[2] when she was simply told to nullify the act abrogating her charter, and to organize government on the old familiar lines " until a governor, of his Majesty's appointment, will consent to govern the colony according to its charter." The Congress could take the more advanced attitude in

[1] *Journal of Congress,* November 3, 5, December 4, 1775.
[2] June 9, 1775, *ibid.*

the later instances because it had the experience of nearly five months to aid it in outlining a policy, and because it regarded itself as the chosen agency of the people, with authority derived from them " according to the purest maxims of representation."[1]

Moreover, with each enlargement of the powers of the Congress, the common aim of a firm union was more nearly consummated. Every increase of the continental army, every act enforcing the Association or regulating trade, every issue of bills of credit, every means toward getting into relations with a foreign power, in short, every one of the countless instances by which it extended its own authority and made it more complex, by so much increased the necessity that this should be done in such manner as would be supported throughout the colonies, and consequently strengthen the union. The political acumen required was of a high order, in that it was necessary not alone to conduct the Congress so as not to get too far ahead of popular opinion, but to keep a guiding hand on the course of events in the colonies as well. This was done through correspondence between the delegates and their constituents, by resolutions of the Congress, and, when the occasion demanded, by personal visits of the members of the Congress.[2]

[1] Declaration of Congress, December 6, 1775, *Journal*.

[2] Notably in the case of sending a committee to New Jersey on December 4, 1775. See below, pp. 45–46.

The union sentiment was greatly fostered by one principle in the conduct of affairs which the Congress followed out with consistent purpose to the end. This was never to perform an act of consequence, nor issue a document designed to influence the popular mind, without stating the causes for it. Statements were invariably so framed as to put the acts of Great Britain always in the wrong, and to make it appear plausible that the course pursued by the Congress was rendered necessary by specified instances of British aggression, coercion, or infringement of what were believed to be undoubted rights, and was the only one possible under the circumstances. Naturally the British side gained nothing by the manner in which it was stated by the Congress. Amid all the vacillation that characterized the earliest period of the activity of the Congress, that is, until the beginning of 1776 (often caused by the very necessity of yielding a little here and a little there, to unite the wishes of individuals and localities in order that the larger movement might not be stayed), this is one point of policy that was carried through with absolute consistency. Consequently, if we search deeply enough, the causal origin of every important resolution or series of resolutions affecting the continental concerns may be found in some previous British action. By carrying out this deep-laid design, confidence was inspired in the minds of the supporters of the Congress, and they were made to believe in its ability and rectitude.

Inseparable from the growth of the authority of the Congress and the resultant strengthening of the union, was the advance toward independence. Before November, 1775, though many acts had been committed that assisted in making the separation inevitable, the Congress can hardly be considered as working consciously to bring about that end. There was too great a want of uniformity of design in its acts, too much of profession of loyalty to Great Britain and denial of any planning for independence, side by side with the passage of resolutions that appear now as having no other possible ultimate conclusion. But this was due to the large conservative element in the Congress, which held the small radical minority strongly in check and forced through concessions. The period between May 10 and November 1, 1775, was one, therefore, which taxed the ingenuity of the members of the Congress to the utmost. For they had to steer a middle course between the desires of the small, aggressive, minority body of radicals on the one side, and those of the large number of conservatives on the other. If they yielded to the former they were in danger of dashing to pieces on the rocks of civil war, if to the latter they might be stranded on the shoals of indecision. There is, therefore, at this time no evidence of a conscious

determination to achieve independence, though
many acts were adopted—notably those relating to
military affairs—which led inevitably in that direction.   The conservatives insisted on sending another petition, in spite of the failure of the first.
This was a wise move, though the full wisdom of it
was not seen even by many of its promoters and opponents.   If the conservatives could, at the price
of agreeing to send another petition, be got to
acquiesce in all the other measures of the Congress, many of them warlike in the extreme and
casting reflection upon all their professions of
loyalty and allegiance to the crown, the cost was not
too great to pay.   If the petition failed, as the radicals all believed it must, and was therefore useless, it was good policy none the less; for it put
the Congress in position to say that it had left no
stone unturned to bring about a peaceful solution
of the controversy, and that no other course was
open except war, for every overture had been rejected.   With the rejection of the petition in
hand the Congress was far stronger before the
country than if none had been sent and no opportunity for rejection given.

Having agreed to send the petition,[1] whatever else
was done, a due and proper period had to be given
for answer to be made.   During the four months

[1] July 8, 1775.

that elapsed before the reply was received, a waiting
policy had to be pursued, and the conservatives saw
to it that no act out of keeping with this policy was
committed.   But this did not prevent the Congress
from fostering the union sentiment in every way
possible. The most important opportunity for doing
this arose out of the indecision of the colonies as
to the course to pursue respecting Lord North's
plan of conciliation and concession.[1]   Three colonies[2] had transmitted the plan to the Congress with
the request for directions as to their conduct respecting it, while the remainder waited, before taking any action, to hear what the Congress would
advise. The reply of the Congress, the last important act before taking a recess during the month of
September, was an unequivocal rejection, and,
though it contained no new thought, was a forcible
statement in denunciation of submission to parliamentary taxation and parliamentary legislation. The
latter point was now carried to its farthermost extreme, and by implication, England's right even
to control the commerce of the colonies upon the
terms stated by the first Congress, and repeated in
the address to the inhabitants of Great Britain,
agreed to on the same day as the petition to the

[1] February 20–27, 1775. Lord North's motion is to be found
in *Journal of Congress,* July 31, 1775.
[2] New Jersey, Pennsylvania, and Virginia.

King, was renounced.[1] No colony gave the resolution further consideration so that this attempt to
break up the union had no other result than to
strengthen it.

The adjournment for the month of August served
the double purpose of enabling the members to return among their constituents, and so keep in
touch with them, and of consuming time while waiting for the reply to the petition to arrive.   When
they reconvened in September[2] no answer had yet
come, and the policy, therefore, had still to be a
waiting one.   The next six weeks are mainly devoted to a consideration of the commerce and trade
of the colonies, and to military affairs, which still
have a defensive cast.   The non-exportation part
of the Association went into effect on September 10.
Appeals to the Congress from various quarters
necessitated some interpretation of its provisions.[3]
No colony would act on its own responsibility.   On
no other point, except in directing military affairs,
was there such general acquiescence in allowing the
Congress a full and free hand.   There was need,
too, that the Congress should express its opinion of

---

[1] July 8, 1775.

[2] September 5, 1775.

[3] See *Journal of Congress,* September 15, 27, 1775; John
Adams' *Works,* II, 451; Diary of Richard Smith, *Am. Hist.
Rev.,* I, 290, 292.

the Restraining Acts[1] of March and April, since
four colonies[2] were favored as against the rest, and
if they took advantage of their exception, they could
break up the union. Though no disposition to do so
was shown, this was a matter of continental concern
and a word from the Congress was awaited. Some
of the radicals would have had the ports opened
to trade with the world at large.[3] But as such a
proposition meant virtual independence it found few
followers. The debate had about run its course
when the announcement was received, on the last
day of October, that not only had the petition been
given no consideration, but that on the very day
when the King was to have received it, he had issued a proclamation declaring the colonists in rebellion. The first reply made by the Congress was
issued the next day. All exportation without the
permission or order of the Congress was to be
stopped until the first of the following March; even
the export of rice, allowed by the provisions of the
Association to be shipped to Great Britain, was prohibited. Further, the four colonies exempted from
the provisions of the Restraining Acts were told not
to avail themselves of the benefits to be derived

[1] The provisions of these acts are given in Chapter XI.
[2] New York, Delaware, North Carolina, and Georgia.
[3] John Adams' *Works*, II, 451–484.

therefrom and were thanked for not having previously done so.[1]

Dating from November first, we can discern the beginning of the conscious movement having independence as its aim.   There was from that time no further talk of petitioning, but there were many expressions within the Congress and many more without that no other course was left, than either to work for independence, or to adopt the impossible alternative of absolute submission and renunciation of all that had been striven for during the past fourteen years.   But in proceeding along the road toward independence as much caution and skill were required as previously had been shown in steering the middle course.   It was necessary never to go a step further than popular opinion could be made to take, and on this account many concessions had to be made to the large body of conservatives within and without the Congress.   In the latter, though their numbers from now on began to decrease, they still held the upper hand and continued to for months to come.

The policy of always putting Great Britain in the wrong and making the acts of the Congress appear as still defensive or retaliatory had to be continued. Though the Congress was unable to go forward with the rapidity that would have pleased the radicals, no

[1] *Journal of Congress,* November 1, 1775.

backward step was taken. For the next month gave
the opportunities for stirring up the democracy
already adverted to,[1] which were eagerly seized upon
as likely to aid the forward movement. The radicals
were for going much further.[2] They would have
taken advantage of the application of New Hampshire, for advice respecting establishing her government, to recommend a general abolition of the old
forms. Fortunately for the success of the revolutionary movement they were not sufficiently strong
to make their opinions prevail, for the Congress as a
body saw that the ground was not yet prepared for
it to act except when appealed to directly. But it
was certainly due to the radicals, and probably as a
concession to them, that the advice given during the
months of November and December had so markedly
a democratic character.

Even so much of progress caused a reaction in
the colonies where the conservative spirit had the
upper hand. The numerous radical expressions,
favoring independence and the adoption of measures
leading thereto, which now (November to December) began to appear in the public prints, caused the
conservatives who still believed there might be some
other way out, to attempt to frustrate the designs of
the radicals. The Pennsylvania conservatives, with

[1] See pp. 33–35.
[2] John Adams' *Works*, III, 19, 20.

Dickinson at their head, were actively supporting
the moderate attitude, all the more because of the
sympathies with the democracy displayed by the
Congress. The salvation of the conservative party
in Pennsylvania depended upon keeping the people,
" the multitude," from getting control of the government there. The old-line conservatives believed
in all sincerity that if the people were allowed to
come into power, nothing short of anarchy would be
the outcome. Dickinson and his followers, controlling Pennsylvania politics, advocated united action
by the colonies, and even fighting for their rights, but
did not favor an aggressive policy. Great as was his
interest in the affairs of the continent, they were to
him secondary to the necessity for preserving the
management of Pennsylvania politics in the hands of
those who had always governed. So much of a desire for independence as was in existence in his
colony at this time was confined, with a few exceptions, to the radicals, who had little share in political
affairs. If they should acquire control, they would
not only overturn the whole fabric of government,
but, by sending representatives of their own views
to the Congress, greatly strengthen the independence
party. This was to be prevented at all hazards, and
one means to this end was to issue new instructions
to Pennsylvania's delegates in the Congress which
would keep them from taking part in any of the

schemes of the radicals, especially such as would change the existing form of the Pennsylvania government.[1] It was fully appreciated, too, that as Pennsylvania led, the other middle colonies where the conservatives were in control, would follow, so that within two months after Pennsylvania's[2] instructions against independence were passed, similar instructions were issued to their delegates by the governing organizations of New Jersey, New York, Delaware and Maryland. One element aiding in the establishment of this attitude, was the hope of the leaders in these colonies that despite the rejection of the petition and the King's proclamation of rebellion, some pressure might still be brought to bear on Parliament to reverse its position. Though the likelihood was not great that such a change of purpose would prevail, the conservatives were for giving a chance of embracing it to the new Parliament, that was to assemble in October.

But the Congress, compelled to listen to instructions against independence, would not sit idly by, if a colony brought up again the idea of sending a

[1] See Lincoln, *Revolutionary Movement in Pennsylvania*, Chap. XII; Reed's *Life and Corr. of Joseph Reed*, and Stillé's *Dickinson*.

[2] Pennsylvania's instructions were issued on November 9; New Jersey's, November 28; New York's on December 14, 1775, and Maryland's, January 11, 1776, though the committee to prepare the last was appointed on December 9, 1775.

petition to the King.   This was no time for further
petitioning, and no such proposition had been made
in the Congress since the last had proved so barren
of results.   Therefore, when New Jersey took up
the matter, there was serious business.   By force of
circumstances it had been necessary to keep hands
off when New York sent her petition some months
back, and for her pains was rewarded by being exempted from the effects of the Restraining Acts.
But now the face of things had changed and a solid
front must be presented at all costs.   A resolution
was passed expressing the view that it would be
" dangerous to the liberties and welfare of America,
if any colony should separately petition the King or
either house of parliament,"[1] and a committee was
appointed to confer with New Jersey on the subject.
Care was taken to put Dickinson, the author of the
last petition of the Congress, at its head.   His com-
panions were Wythe and Jay, a radical and a conservative, and their efforts were so successful as
to cause New Jersey to abandon all thought of sending a new petition.   If New Jersey had not yielded
so promptly to this gentle persuasion, there is no
doubt that stronger measures, even to the employment of force, would have been resorted to to overthrow its government.[2]

[1] *Journal of Congress,* December 4, 1775.
[2] *New Jersey Archives,* 1st Series, X, 677–678, 689–691;
Force, 4th, III, 1871–1874.

Almost a month had passed since the Congress had obtained official information of the failure of its petition, and no statement had been issued in reply. It was time, therefore, to speak out, the more so as Lord Howe had also published a proclamation prohibiting the people of Boston from leaving the town without permission. The answer to these was made on December 6, in a proclamation sent forth in the name of " the delegates of the thirteen United Colonies of North America," and the most defiant of all the documents so far emanating from the Congress. All allegiance to Parliament is specifically disavowed, even that to the King is brought into question somewhat in the argument. And in reply to that part of the King's proclamation announcing the punishment to be meted out to those caught aiding and abetting the rebellion, the Congress boldly announces that it will retaliate in kind and degree. All this is done " in the name of the people of the United Colonies, and by authority, according to the purest maxims of representation." No convention or committee is to intervene to aid in carrying out this threat, Congress itself assumes the burden and will bear it. This is the highest point of authority which the Congress had yet reached, but, since in the last resort military force would be invoked, it could thus speak out without exciting the jealousy of any colony.

The last two months of the year 1775 saw many
acts committed by the Congress that occasioned an
increase of its power, and at the same time strengthened the union and made for independence.   The
beginnings were made in three points of sovereign
policy that ultimately had far reaching consequences.
These were the initial attempts at suppressing the
loyalist sympathizers; the first steps toward inviting
foreign intervention; and those toward laying the
foundations of a continental navy.[1]   Along with
these is to be noticed a far stiffer tone in military
affairs, and less talk of acting only on the defensive,
the while actions were belying professions.   All
these acts paved the way for the more vigorous policy that was to be ushered in with the New Year.
After November there begins a gradual weakening
of the power of the conservatives, and we see devel-
oping the conscious aim toward independence.   The
end of the waiting policy that had characterized the
proceedings of the previous five months was at hand.
For two months at least the advance is not rapid,
but after that it gets full headway and goes forward
with a rush that nothing can stop.   Every act that
can foster it is committed, and every opposition to
it is borne down, by gentle means if possible, by force
if necessary.   By each step the authority of the

[1] The issuance of bills of credit may also be regarded as
tending in this direction.

Congress is increased, the necessity for united action made more urgent, and the sentiment for declaring independence so aroused, that he who is not for it is made to appear as an enemy of his country.

4

CHAPTER III

THE IDEA OF INDEPENDENCE TAKES ROOT, AND THE CONGRESS PREVAILS

At the opening of the most notable year in American history, though the radical advocates of an independence policy had made much progress in perfecting the revolutionary organization, they had not succeeded in winning to their support any considerable numbers in the Congress. But a scant third of the thirty-five or forty men, controlling the political destinies of the colonies, were as yet open advocates of measures leading to a definitive break with the home government. So strong was the conservative spirit still prevailing that of them all one colony alone, Virginia, could at a roll call muster a majority of her delegates on the side of an avowal of independence.[1] The conservative majority, still favored a waiting policy, with military movements mainly of defensive character ; a course rendered the more necessary by the failure of several colonies[2] to keep delegations in Congress sufficiently large to enable them to cast a vote. But the current be-

[1] See pp. 84–85.
[2] North Carolina and Georgia were not represented at this time, nor South Carolina for a brief period a little later on.

gan to set more strongly in the direction of independence as each day passed. The public prints throughout the colonies were beginning to contain, more and more, arguments favoring it, while in their private correspondence the leaders of thought, who were also prolific contributors to the gazettes, were more outspoken than they dared be in public. At the same time, there is discernible a constant increase in the power and authority of the Congress, made necessary by the more offensive character which the war gradually assumed, and the resultant change in the nature of the struggle. The Congress came to be accepted generally as the directing head of affairs, "the supreme superintending power,"[1] and each extension of jurisdiction was so skilfully managed as to meet with welcome as the logical outcome of events.

The time was ready for some event that would give impetus to the thought that independence was inevitable, and, by playing into the hands of the Congress, give the opportunity to direct affairs with the purpose of achieving independence in mind, to be carried through by the constant extension of its own authority. To the good fortune of the revolutionary movement, the uprising in America had led the King to call Parliament to meet on October 26, 1775, to consider the situation. In his brief speech on

[1] *Rhode Island Col. Records,* VII, 448–449.

opening the session he left no doubt as to the force
of his determination.   The colonies were in rebellion, he declared, and were conspiring, in spite of
their outspoken protests to the contrary, to establish
an independent government.   To prevent this all
the resources of the British empire would be drawn
on if necessary, and as a first step the army and navy
had been increased. Also " most friendly offers of
foreign assistance" had been received, and his
Electoral troops had been sent to the garrisons
of Gibraltar and Port Mahon, in order to free the
British troops of these garrisons for service elsewhere.   In closing he made reference to the intention to give power to agents on the spot, to grant
pardons and to receive the submission of such
provinces and colonies as were disposed to return
to their allegiance.[1]   Though rumors were current
in America before the year 1775 was out, that a
speech of this nature had been delivered by the
King, the speech itself did not reach Boston until
the fourth of January, and Philadelphia until three
days later.   On the eighth it was known by every
man in the Congress, as also that large reinforcements to the British army had arrived, and that
Norfolk had been destroyed by Lord Dunmore.
On the next day Paine's *Common Sense* made its
appearance.

[1] *Force,* 4th, VI, 1.

Such a favorable concurrence of historical accidents was of inestimable value to the radical side. The King's speech and the burning of Norfolk were welcomed as grist for their mill, for which *Common Sense* furnished the much needed propelling force. No arguments from the leaders were so convincing, as the sight of a substantial town in ashes, the news that the British redcoats would overrun the land, and that a British navy would invest it from the sea. But even these, in view of the King's proposal to send agents to America with power to act, might have failed to stir up the dissatisfied elements, if *Common Sense* had not made its appearance. It is no longer necessary to enter into details respecting its vast influence. All scholars are at one in giving this unusual pamphlet credit for a large share in the popularization of the newly arisen ideas of independence, and, in a measure, for shaping the whole movement. But its influence would not have been so great had it not been published at so opportune a time.

And the thought therefore arises, is it likely that such a pamphlet, which was a considerable time in preparation, and with whose author many of the men of the Congress were on terms of familiar relation, was sent out on its message at this precise time by grace of providential dispensation? We know well that the men who were controlling the revolu-

tionary movement were far-seeing statesmen, many
of them, unaccustomed and unwilling to trust vital
affairs to the uncertain favors of fortune. They
were naturally keen to take advantage of every
means that might aid them, for their lives and fortunes were staked with their reputations. So far,
on the part of the Congress in its official documents,
there had been a distinct disavowal of any purposed
striving for independence, though its acts were
hardly always in keeping with its avowals. The
conservatives, still in control, saw to it that no other
policy was pursued. But in the aggressive minority,
among whom Franklin was an active spirit, were
those who were working to influence public opinion
in the direction of independence, thereby aiming to
react on the Congress itself. For it was perfectly
understood that, though the Congress should be always kept a little ahead of the trend of the popular
ideas, and outline the course of action, it must do
this in so subtle a manner as never to appear actually to lead, merely to direct. Since the early part
of November the more radical spirits had decided
that independence was the goal to strive for. Particularly with the view of breaking up the old conservative party in Pennsylvania, it is altogether
probable that Franklin, with the connivance of
others of his way of thinking, made preparation to
further their side of the cause by having a pamphlet

written which could be used to counteract the effects
of the King's speech, or any measures that Parliament might adopt, in the unlikely event that they
would be conciliatory, and to fan the flame of dis-
content if they were of the character they proved
to be.   The date of the meeting of Parliament was
well known in America, as also the fact that it took
about two months for information to reach from
the other side.   Paine was accordingly employed,
in the autumn of 1775, to write a pamphlet which
might be issued at nearly the same time as the first
news of the proceedings in Parliament was made
known, and thereby aid those who were now the
avowed advocates of an independence policy, and
who still had the inertia of the conservatives to
overcome.   The preparation of *Common Sense* was
conceived with deliberation, and for a definite object.
It would have appeared about this time had there
been no speech from the King.   But the large measure of its success, was due to the careful foresight
that caused its preparation for publication at the
psychological moment best calculated to give it currency, and render it of most effect in shaping
opinion.[1]

Its appearance, too, was intimately associated
with the contest going on in Pennsylvania, in whose

[1] For the details respecting the negotiations with Paine see
Conway's *Life of Paine.*

affairs the Congress found opportunity to take ever greater and greater part. The radicals by reason of the share they were having in raising troops, were gaining largely in power though still unable to direct affairs. Franklin had allied himself with them, and was a powerful factor on their side. They were now making such rapid strides as to be held in check with ever increasing difficulty. Unquestionably, because of his desire to influence opinion in Pennsylvania in favor of the moderates, James Wilson, on the very day that *Common Sense* appeared, made his motion that the Congress issue an address in reply to the King's speech, wherein denial should be made that the colonies were aiming at independence, and should " declare to their constituents and the World their present intentions respecting an Independency."[1] His motion, though strongly supported, was under the rules postponed, and another day assigned for its consideration. When taken up again on the twenty-fourth, it was passed, and a conservative committee[2] was selected to prepare the

[1] *Diary of Richard Smith,* January 9, 1776, *American Hist. Rev.,* I, No. 2, 307. For a lucid account of the complex political struggle in Pennsylvania, see Lincoln's *The Revolutionary Movement in Pennsylvania.*

[2] The committee consisted of Dickinson, Wilson, Hooper, Duane, and Alexander. The *Address* as reported is among the Papers of the Continental Congress, and is entirely in Wilson's handwriting. It has been printed in *Am. Hist. Rev.,* I, 684–696.

address. And, as if wishing to make display of the ultimate futility of such procedure, its opponents were on the very same day sufficiently powerful to have a committee appointed to consider the equally important matter of the propriety of establishing a war office.   Three weeks passed before Wilson was ready with his address, which Richard Smith describes as " very long, badly written, and full against Independency."[1]

But in these three weeks events had moved rapidly, and the Congress was now in no mood to listen to, much less adopt and issue such a document as expressing its attitude.   The military measures made necessary by the fall of Quebec and the death of Montgomery ; the general quickening of mind and act that they had brought about ; the resolutions adopted to suppress Tories ; the rumors that foreign troops were to be engaged by Great Britain for service in America ; the constantly recurring arguments in the gazettes favoring independence, all combined to render it unlikely that the Congress would now stop to issue any pronouncement on the subject of independence, and least of all one putting it in opposition to a course which it was tacitly favoring on every possible occasion.   But an element aiding in the defeat of Wilson's proposal that must not be ignored, was the arrival of two new

[1] *Diary,* February 13, 1776.

delegations from New England, and of Chase of
Maryland.   Fresh from home they could tell of the
spirit animating the people, and in their journeying
to the Congress had the opportunity to get in touch
with public sentiment from Boston to Baltimore.
Sherman, Wolcott, and Huntington of Connecticut
arrived on January 16, Chase about February 3,
and John Adams and Gerry of Massachusetts on
February 9.   The last two together with Samuel
Adams now formed a majority of the Massachusetts
delegation, and could therefore completely control
the vote of that colony.   As the Connecticut delegates were not less ardently radical in their views
than those of Massachusetts, together they had great
weight in determining the course of events, both
by argument and by the example of their vote,
winning over a majority of the colonies.   They
opposed all measures that obstructed independence,
and though as yet unable to dominate completely
the actions of the Congress, they of course stood in
the way of the adoption and issuance of Wilson's
proposed address.   Able support was received, too,
from Franklin and Chase, who, though bound by
instructions against voting for independence, worked
to further every measure that might bring it about.
As the result of their combined activities and exertions, the address, after its report to the Congress,
is not heard of again.   If the radicals could not force

the Congress to advance, at least they could prevent any backward step from being taken. And the noticeable stiffening of the attitude of the Congress, which dates from this period, is in large measure due to the influence exerted by these two new delegations, whose persistency in turn brought about a gradual accession of numbers to their ranks. Both the Adamses were working strenuously also, without the doors of the Congress, to make converts to their views. Samuel Adams bent his energies upon arousing the democracy of Pennsylvania, and began to contribute arguments favoring independence to the Philadelphia newspapers. These were much needed, particularly in Philadelphia, where in spite of the presence of the Congress a strong conservative element still held predominance.

A further insight into the increasing strength of the more advanced party is obtained, from a view of the incidents happening about the same time and attending the oration delivered by the Reverend Doctor William Smith on the occasion of the public services, held by order of the Congress, in memory of the death of General Montgomery. Smith's oration, breathing throughout its length the spirit of loyalty and allegiance to the King, was little to the liking of the majority of the Congress who, while not seeing their way clear to announcing independence, listened with scant patience to a preaching

about their duty as loyal subjects of King George.
Accordingly, when a few days later William Livingston moved that a vote of thanks be extended to
Doctor Smith with a request that he print his oration, it was objected to because the " Dr. declared
the sentiments of the Congress to continue in a
Dependency on Great Britain which Doctrine the
Congress cannot now approve."[1]   To every one
approving Livingston's proposition two voices spoke
against it, and so strong was the opposition, that fore-
seeing failure, he withdrew the motion.   The main
value of this occurrence lies in the light it throws
upon the attitude of the Congress as a body toward
independence.   The leading speakers and writers
were advocating the adoption of measures leading to
it at every opportunity, and so unimportant an episode as the introduction of Livingston's motion, was
not allowed to pass before Chase, John Adams,
Wythe, Edward Rutledge, Wolcott, and Sherman
had given expression to their views against it.   The
nature of the instructions of five colonies to their
delegates, however, acted as an estoppel upon their
assenting to any open avowal in favor of independence.   Until they were withdrawn or revised, these
delegations could not vote for any measure having
independence as its object.   But this did not prevent
them as individuals from speaking and working

[1] *Diary of Richard Smith,* February *21, 1776.*

for it, so long as they halted short of casting the
vote of their colony contrary to instructions.

In the six or seven weeks that intervened between
the arrival of the King's speech and the two occasions on which the Congress uttered its opposition
to taking any action that would stand in the way of
ultimate independence, *Common Sense* was being
disseminated throughout the land, ably supported
by productions of lesser distinction, many taking
their cue from it.   The people were growing familiar gradually with the thought of an independent government, and the Congress, marvelously in
touch with every phase of this development, kept
pace with it.   So that by the end of February, the
question in the minds of many of those in the Congress who are still to be classed as conservatives,
was not one of the advisability or inadvisability of
independence, but of the means and measures by
which it should be brought about; of the prepara-
tions that should be made in advance of its declaration, and above all of the readiness of the people for
it.   For without the support of the democracy the
whole of the revolutionary organizations would
collapse.   These, it is true, were being strengthened
with every increase in the continental army, but
even the lengths which the Congress could go in
adding to it, depended entirely upon the extent to
which the populace would follow in enlisting for

the armed struggle.   The Congress had thus all the
while to feel its way and, by keeping in careful
touch with the people, to know how far it might
advance.

Yet, notwithstanding the many arguments that
had appeared favoring independence, and the almost
equally frequent advocacy of opening the ports of
the country to trade with the world, as a preliminary
step, many still had misgivings, and until these
were overcome any too radical action might compass the downfall of the whole movement.   Combined with the natural disinclination from the overturn of a constitutional authority that had always
been recognized in some form, and which, even the
most radical admitted, conferred mutual advantages
of no mean order, was that other deterring element,
of aversion at the thought of the cost at which independence of England might be procured.   Would
not after all more be lost thereby than by continuing
the attempt at obtaining the desired reforms within
the empire?   What guarantees could be offered that
they would have more liberty under a new order
than under the old?   Would they ever be able to
stand alone?   Was there not danger, if they brought
about a separation from England, that another
power, France, the traditional enemy, might step in
and take advantage of their weakness for her own
aggrandizement?   As has been well said, "so strong

was the love for the old country, so great was the
pride of being a part of the British dominion, and
entitled to the glories of her history, that many
shrank from an explicit recognition and declaration
of the fact that the colonies were indeed independent
States, no longer a part of their old country." [1]
Thoughts such as these coursed through the minds
of many, giving them pause, and were as often the
considerations blocking hasty action in Virginia and
South Carolina, as in more conservative Pennsylvania and New York. Numbers were unwilling to
take the final leap until they had carefully gone over
the ground on which they would alight, and were
assured that it was not sown with pitfalls.

The vague mention in the King's speech, of his
intention to send to America agents with indefinite
power to accommodate the differences, and this too
in despite of the not uncertain character of the remainder of the speech, fostered markedly this reluctant sentiment, both within and without the
Congress. There was a very wide diffusion of the
idea that all radical measures should halt until the
opportunity was given to learn something definite
about these " commissioners," as they were very
generally called.[2] The discerning Joseph Reed
could not fail to wonder at the " strange reluctance

---

[1] McCrady, *South Carolina in the Revolution,* 175–176.
[2] Stevens' *Facsimiles,* 890[1].

in the minds of many to cut the knot." " Though
no man of understanding expects any good from the
commissioners, yet they are for waiting to hear their
proposals before they declare off." This was particularly the case in Pennsylvania " and to the south-
ward."[1]

That a bill embracing the clause authorizing the
appointment of such a commission was under consideration and likely to pass, was known in America
in the early part of February. Some of the very
persons active in perfecting the revolutionary organizations were influenced by the possibilities for
reconciliation that might lie with these commissioners. Wordy discussions respecting their aims and
their powers for good and evil, filled the gazettes
during the months of March and April. One of the
principal arguments hurled against waiting to hear
the propositions that they might have to make, was
that they would be similar to Lord North's conciliatory motion of the year before, designed merely
to divide the colonies by playing off one against the
other. The correspondence of every man of importance contains some reference to these expected
agents of conciliation, and they are all in agreement
upon their effect in blocking the independence movement. Washington had no patience with the
thought of waiting for them and considered the idea

[2] Reed's *Reed*, I, 163, March 3, 1776.

as insulting as Lord North's motion.[1] Reed was more in fear of them than of the British generals and armies. He was fearful " if their propositions are plausible, and behaviour artful," that they would " divide us." " There is so much suspicion in Congress," he informed Washington, "and so much party on this subject, that very little more fuel is required to kindle the flame."[2] John Adams of course placed no store by them, " a messiah that will never come," and he " laughed, . . . scolded, . . . grieved and . . . rip'd " at the story of their coming, and stormed against what he termed " as arrant an illusion as ever was hatched in the brain of an enthusiast, a politician, or a maniac.'[3] The views of the more conservative members of the Congress are well expressed in a letter of Thomas Stone, of Maryland. " If the Commissioners do not arrive shortly and conduct themselves with great candor and uprightness," he wrote towards the end of April to Jenifer, " to effect a reconciliation, a separation will most undoubtedly take place." He wished " to conduct affairs so that a just & honorable reconciliation should take place, or that we should be pretty unanimous in a resolution to fight it out for Independence. . . ."[4]

[1] Reed's *Reed*, I, 170.   [2] *Ibid.*, I, 173.
[3] *Letters to his Wife*, I, 98.
[4] *Journal and Corr. Md. Council of Safety*, 383.

5

Anxiously on the lookout for any sign that might indicate a show of a conciliatory spirit on the part of Great Britain, all those not already committed to independence pinned their hopes to these commissioners. But as days and weeks went by and their arrival was delayed, and rumors about them still remained indefinite and conflicting, even those most sanguine in the expectation of the good they would accomplish gradually lost confidence, and listened to the persuasive oratory of those who placed no trust in either the commissioners or their mission. After the momentous month of March those who still had faith in commissioners were inconsiderable in numbers and devoid of influence. After the sixth of May,[1] until independence was already more than two months old, no attention was again given to them. And when they finally arrived and negotiations with them were begun, the unsatisfactory powers with which they were clothed, and the new spirit infused by the fact that independence had been declared, rendered the negotiations abortive.

But no one influence was of such effect in silencing those who still advocated further temporizing, and in convincing them that longer delay on the score of prospective commissioners was useless, as the information which reached America early in May, that Great Britain had actually engaged for-

[1] See *Journal of Congress,* May 6, 1776.

eign mercenaries, then on their way over sea, to fight her battles in America.[1] Up till now there had been many vague rumors floating about respecting England's bid for Russians and Hessians and Hanoverians, but nothing specific had been learned. The thought that England would be forced to seek outside aid was of early origin,[2] and that application had been made to Russia with no success was known in America early in December. In January information more definite was obtained from the reference to offers of foreign assistance in the King's speech. And throughout the next three months the pamphleteers let pass no opportunity to harp upon this additional witness to England's cruel intentions. When, therefore, on May 10,[3] unquestioned evidence was put before the eyes of the Congress that 12,000 Hessians were about to be sent on their way, nay, were even then at sea, the effect in vivifying the acts of the Congress was, in its intensity, unequaled by any occurrence since the arrival of the King's speech four months before.

In order to preserve a continuity of narrative, it has been necessary to run a little ahead and pass

[1] The story of the British negotiations for foreign assistance has been often told; the details can be found in Bancroft, Chapters L and LVII.

[2] See *Force,* 4th, III, 819, 944, 1592.

[3] *Journal of Congress.* Thos. Cushing's letter conveying the intelligence is to be found in *Force,* 4th, V, 1184.

by some affairs in which the constantly increasing
authority of the Congress is displayed.   Of these
none is more important than the regulation of the
colonial commercial relations.   From the day that
the Articles of Association went into effect, the
Congress was the recognized interpreter for the
continent in all affairs having to do with its foreign
commerce.   The view was general that this affair
was the Congress's; that its importance to the welfare of America was such that no colony could act
solely on its own responsibility; that all must conduct themselves in this respect in accordance with
the rules laid down by the general body.   Because
of this the power and jurisdiction of the Congress
were extended, and its influence came to be felt far
and wide.   Where so many were merchants and
traders, when such numbers found the advance of
their interests, even their means of existence, dependent upon a word from the Congress, that body
found it could keep in close touch with the economic
life of the continent, by the control of its trade.
The influence, therefore, was reciprocal: the people,
acting through the assemblies, the conventions, the
committees of safety, looked to the Congress for
direction; the Congress in turn gave this in accordance with the best light it had.   And by a judicious
permission granted now here, now there, to break
its own rules, it did much to relieve the severity of

the non-intercourse agreement and to establish itself, not as a mere autocratic dictator, but rather as the mild ruler acting for the good of all, upon consultation with all, and after careful consideration of all interests involved. When the day came finally for declaring the ports open to trade with all parts of the world,[1] the Congress with one stroke abolished one of the most potent means it had established for maintaining dominance in continental affairs. By that time there was no need to adopt measures designed merely to increase its power. It was strong enough to do practically anything it willed, short of declaring independence. And the energies of all the aggressive members were henceforth bent upon forcing through independence and creating a military organization that could support it when declared.

The ink was scarcely dry on the trade compromise of November first[2] when exceptions to its general provisions were found to be necessary, and during the next four months these increased with the pass of every day. But however much these infractions of its rules, made under the Congress's own authority, differed in character, they had all the same end in view: to procure arms, ammunition, and other much-needed warlike supplies.[3] Throughout, the

[1] April 6, 1776.
[2] See pp. 41–42.
[3] *Journal of Congress,* November 22, December 11, 14, 1775.

attitude of the Congress is far bolder than is assumed on other occasions, and a dictatorial tone is adopted repeatedly. Though it left the enforcement of its resolutions to the assemblies, conventions, and committees of safety, the Congress fixed the terms under which individuals might be permitted to export; the amount and character of the bonds to be entered and to whom to be given; the tonnage of the cargoes, and the destination of the vessels; the time and place of sailing, and the period within which, as evidence of good faith, return must be made to some friendly American port. Unless these stipulations were complied with in advance, no permits to trade were issued. And the Congress was careful to state, in several cases, that the permission was by reason of particular circumstances, and was not to be " drawn into precedent," thus leaving open the door for refusal when it deemed such action wise.[1]

But the time was approaching (March 1) when, unless some other action was taken, the ports under the terms of the Articles of Association would be opened, and trade with Great Britain might be resumed. The first two months of the new year saw consideration given to this knotty problem whenever the other multifarious questions which so en-

[1] *Journal of Congress*, December 15, 1775, January 27, February 2, 1776.

grossed the attention of the Congress allowed. Earnest and serious discussion of the question began in the middle of February. By that time the public prints were teeming with all manner of arguments favoring and opposing independence. And the reiterated advocacy of open ports and free trade with all parts of the world, now in conjunction with independence, again as a precedent to it, did much to reassure those in Congress who favored the most radical measures. It was well understood that open ports and independence were inseparably connected, but the conservatives were not yet ready for this step. For such action meant the nullification by act of the Congress of the various trade laws enacted by the Parliament of England.

Towards the end of February, it was seen that no conclusion could be reached before the first of March, and inasmuch as merchants in Philadelphia and elsewhere were preparing to make the most of their opportunities beginning with March first, recourse was had to another temporary expedient. On the twenty-sixth of February it was resolved that no vessel laden for Great Britain, Ireland, or the West Indies should be permitted to sail without further order of the Congress, and the committees of inspection and observation were called on to see to the enforcement of this resolution. The very next day Robert Morris came into the Congress

bearing in his hand the " very long and cruel "[1] act
prohibiting trade and intercourse with America,
which had been signed by the King on December
22, 1775. This put a new face on affairs. The
first reply was issued on the fourth of March, when
the resolution of the twenty-sixth of February was
rescinded, and trade with Great Britain and Ireland
and the British West Indies was legalized, if engaged in for the purpose of procuring arms and
ammunition.

These were the days, it will be remembered, when
there was still much talk of commissioners and the
good that might flow from them. But when the
very act which made provision for their appointment
was found to contain clauses which authorized the
British officers and seamen to share in the prizes
which they captured, and to seize and force to serve
under the British flag all persons found on board
these ships, a resentful desire to retaliate in kind
took the place of the patient waiting upon the hoped-
for chance of reconciliation with Great Britain.
The next few weeks were big with events of the
greatest importance to America. The radicals were
growing more and more aggressive, and as each suc-
cessive act was disclosed, showing the unconcilia-
tory spirit of Great Britain, the conservatives had
the ground more and more cut from under them.

[1] *Diary of Richard Smith, Am. Hist. Rev.,* I, 506.

On the twenty-third of March the first real reply
to the Prohibitory Act was made in the resolutions
authorizing the equipment of privateers. Almost
immediately the details providing how these resolutions were to be carried into effect were passed, the
Congress in every particular demonstrating its authority over those who would take advantage of the
privileges now allowed. Within a few days there
was general exultation throughout the land over the
evacuation of Boston, and almost equal dejection
was occasioned by the news that foreign troops
were being hired by England for service in America.
The Congress, taking advantage of the general and
widely diffused enthusiasm aroused by Washington's success, felt that the time had come when,
without losing prestige among the people, it could
adopt a measure that from the point of view of independence was the most important yet passed.
Therefore, on April 6, the ports of the colonies were
thrown open to trade to all parts of the world, except Great Britain. But in so doing the Congress
also reserved the right to enact any commercial
regulations that future necessity might require, re-
enacted those parts of the Association not incon-
sistent with the new resolutions, made recommendations to the colonies as to the manner of enforcing
these regulations, directed the seizure of all goods
imported from British dominions, and prohibited

absolutely the importation of slaves.[1]   Thus was
ended the contest that had been on for three months.

The extent of the power and authority which the
Congress had acquired, is demonstrated by the passing and the general support accorded this act,
whereby virtually one of the most powerful means
for controlling general continental affairs was given
up. Its jurisdiction in respect of trade had till now
been maintained, and through it the Congress could
influence colonial action and keep in touch with the
condition of public thought throughout the country.
But the question henceforth was not one of acquir-
ing additional powers, but of forcing through a
unanimous resolution of independence.

The while this discussion over the issuance of
some public announcement respecting trading with
foreign countries was under consideration, the Congress was secretly planning to carry on such trade
on its own account, intent upon procuring from
abroad, notably from France, all manner of warlike
supplies, though it veiled its intentions under the
guise of procuring articles suitable for the Indians.[2]

As early as the nineteenth of February a contract
had been entered into with Silas Deane to engage in
an enterprise of this nature, to carry out which two

[1] *Journal of Congress,* April 6, 1776.
[2] *Deane Papers* (N. Y. Hist. Soc.), I, 116; *Journal of Congress,* January 27, 1776.

hundred thousand dollars was put at the disposal of the committee having the matter in charge. From them Deane received his instructions upon the first of March. Within the next two days the Committee of Secret Correspondence gave him credentials to go to France " there to transact such Business, commercial and political as we have committed to his Care, in Behalf and by Authority of the Congress of the thirteen united Colonies," and provided him with elaborate instructions how to enter into negotiations with the French government.[1]

If we examine the personnel of the committee having charge of the relations of the colonies with foreign countries, the Committee of Secret Correspondence as it was called, we discover one of the most interesting facts that a close study of any of the affairs of this period discloses. Of the five members composing the committee, three, Franklin, Dickinson, and Morris, were from Pennsylvania. Harrison was from Virginia, and Jay represented New York. Strangely enough, no New England member was added to the committee until many days after independence had been declared. Moreover, of this committee Franklin was the only openly avowed radical. Harrison, to say the least, had decided conservative proclivities, while Dickinson, Morris, and Jay were the most forceful leaders on

[1] *Deane Papers*, 117–119, 123 *et seq.*

the conservative side. They were the ardent opponents of every measure that appeared to have independence for its object, and until the restrictions which their respective colonies had placed upon their actions respecting independence, were removed, their voice and vote were always in opposition. And yet, in secret, they were willing to make themselves parties to a policy that had as its aim the nullification of British laws respecting the colonies, a policy that was more nearly allied to actual independence than anything previously undertaken by act of the Congress, and to do this a month in advance of the time when the Congress adopted the first of its most radical resolutions. This discloses their real attitude, therefore, not only to independence, but to the colonies which they represented. Moreover it demonstrates how necessary it was, before independence could be made an accomplished fact, to have the instructions against independence repealed. Perfectly willing to do secretly what they dared not do openly, the actions of these men have the appearance of inconsistency. But they become quite comprehensible when we bear in mind the local conditions which colored all their public acts.

CHAPTER IV

The Congress and the Democracy

The Congress was the representative of the colonies, in a way having some of the attributes of our Senate. The members were elected, not directly by the people, but by what then corresponded to the legislatures of our day—the conventions or provincial congresses or assemblies. They were, therefore, under the control of these revolutionary political organizations and responsible to them. When, therefore, an election to the Congress was accepted, the delegate was of necessity bound by whatever instructions it was thought meet and proper to give him. Until these were withdrawn they must be followed, no matter what individual opinions were held. It was consequently impossible for the delegations representing New York, Pennsylvania, Delaware, Maryland, or New Jersey, to cast their votes in favor of independence until new instructions were issued to them rescinding the old.[1] In fact it was with difficulty that they could be persuaded to support the resolutions for issuing letters of marque and reprisal[2] and open-

[1] For prior reference to these instructions see p. 45.
[2] March 23, 1776, *Journal of Congress.*

ing the ports, for their radical character was well appreciated. But for doing this they could plead extenuation in the harsh terms of the Prohibitory Act, and they took the chances that their action would meet with the support of their constituents, now flushed by the success at Boston, though the delegates had many misgivings as to the nature of the reception their decidedly conservative communities would accord such radical measures.

During the next three months,[1] the aggressive radicals bent their energies toward compelling the colonies to withdraw their anti-independence instructions, and lost no opportunity to further their ends. With the possible exception of New York, no colony had been more persistent in maintaining the old order than Pennsylvania, and into the political upheaval going on in that colony the Congress was about to project itself with vigor, knowing full well that if Pennsylvania could be brought into line, the cause was won, for she still controlled the policy of the middle colonies.

John Jay, not less than John Dickinson and Robert Morris, represented the old-line aristocrats whose ascendancy in New York, as in Pennsylvania, was being undermined by the rise to power of the democracy. These men were not a whit less patriots, in the sense current at that time, than Franklin or

[1] April, May, and June.

the Adamses or Jefferson. But independence meant
to the former the overthrow of the administrative
organizations with which they had always been
allied, and which saw to it that the democracy was
held in check. They had been among the leaders
in disseminating ideas of the rights of man and of
the equality of men, and in so doing were perfectly
consistent. These abstract theories, as they viewed
it, were to serve as a basis for stating the American
attitude in the controversy with England. Little
thought had been given to their possible application
to conditions in the colonies, and to their destructive
effect upon conservative traditions. But when the
people at large had been fed for ten years and more
upon such a diet, and, moreover, were called upon to
enlist and fight for the rights which they had been
led to believe were theirs, what more natural than
that they should demand their full share when the
time came for distribution? Upon their shoulders,
in large measure, rested the burden of the war, and
they would dictate how it was to be carried.

Consequently, in an especial degree in the middle
colonies, but to no less an extent in South Carolina,[1]
political revolutions were taking place side by side
with the larger struggle, in which all were concerned

---

[1] See the notable study of Dr. Wm. A. Schaper on *Section-
alism and Representation in S. C.* in *Rep. Am. Hist. Assn.*,
1900, Vol. I, especially pp. 338 *et seq.* and 354 *et seq.*

alike. The democracy was fighting there not only
for the general cause, but for itself, and the peaceful
clashes between radicals and conservatives, though
little less frequent and determined, are not heard in
the din of the rattle of musketry and the roar of
artillery. But unless they be taken into account a
full appreciation of the motives underlying the
retarding influences on independence cannot be obtained. The contest for independence in its later
stages, that is just before July 4, 1776, in Pennsylvania, New Jersey, North and South Carolina, and to
almost an equal extent in New York, Delaware,
and Maryland, became virtually not less one between the people and the aristocrats for control,
than one between the United Colonies and Great
Britain for the establishment of a separate government. In all of these contests the influence of the
Congress, whenever possible, was cast on the side
of the democracy. The early sympathy displayed
with it in November and December, in the resolutions advising New Hampshire, South Carolina, and
Virginia to establish governments by calling a " full
and free representation of the people," though not
going so far as a few extreme radicals desired,[1]
went too far for the conservatives. In the reaction

---

[1] John Adams would have had the Congress issue instructions to all the colonies to form new governments. See pp.
34–35, 43, *supra*.

that followed (in bringing about which Dickinson
was the prime mover) instructions were issued to
the delegations of five colonies preventing them
from assenting to any resolutions favoring independence.   These were designed as much to prevent the
overthrow of the existing governmental machinery
still in conservative control, as to bind the hand
of the Congress.   For it was well understood that
if independence were declared, each colony would
of necessity have to devise a new form of government.   In this process the conservatives feared that
the democracy might gain the upper hand, and overturn the old established order, and the wisdom of
their caution was justified by subsequent events.

But the Congress, a revolutionary organization,
itself in large measure the creature of the democratic revolutionary organizations, had no occasion
to stand in fear of the people.   In fact the radicals
in the Congress saw clearly that dependence must in
the main be placed upon them.   And as the conservatives could control the votes of only five
colonies (the votes being always taken by colonies
and not by individuals), they could not hold the
radicals in check when there was a full representation
of the colonies in the Congress.[1]   Accordingly the

[1] The Congress was always a fluctuating body, and in the
last months of 1775 and the first months of 1776, when affairs
at home were of extreme importance, members came and
went constantly, so that frequently a colony was not represented.

6

Congress took advantage of every occasion that offered to stir up the democracy, and this phe-nomenon of a representative body taking more radical action than a number of its constituent parts would have had it, is one of the interesting develop-ments of the time. It serves also to show the com-plex nature of the controversy.

The measures the Congress resorted to in order to accomplish its ends were various. Perhaps that of most consequence was the increase of the continental army, judiciously distributed throughout the colo-nies, now by request, again as the exigencies made requisite. Through it the Congress made its own existence a real entity, and supported the often weak revolutionary organizations. Philadelphia was a great distance from the seat of many of the colonial activities, and news traveled with painful slowness. The presence, therefore, of the army, the outward demonstration of the majesty and power of the Con-gress, had an effect in overawing the opposition to it that is not now easily discernible, though not less potent on that account. When the Congress saw fit to take measures to support the weak credit of its issues of paper money,[1] to promote the signing of associations, or to suppress the activities of Tories, the continental army was ready to hand to assist, if the committees of safety were inclined to call

[1] *Journal of Congress,* January 11, 1776.

upon it.[1] When, by taking part in the Pennsyl-
vania-Connecticut dispute at Wyoming, it could let
the dissatisfied elements of the western counties of
Pennsylvania know that their interests were being
guarded by it, the Congress did not hesitate to project itself into this controversy, even though it
thereby aroused the resentment of the Pennsylvania
Assembly. But the Congress, bent on establishing
itself with the people, cared little for this Assembly,
controlled as it was by the aristocrats who could be
moved only by force, and ignored its existence consistently from the day that the Pennsylvania Committee of Safety came into power. When the committee was sent to Canada in the hope that the people
of that country might be induced to join their forces
in the struggle, they were authorized to explain
the " method of collecting the sense of the People,
and conducting our Affairs regularly by Committees
of Observation and Inspection in the several Districts, and by Conventions and Committees of
Safety in the several Colonies." And they were
further to " press them to have a complete representation of the People assembled in Convention,
with all possible expedition, to deliberate concern-

[1] *Ibid.*, January 2, 3, 5, 30, February 5, 8, March 8, 9, 14.
In one instance this was done, however, without any reference
to any committee of safety, assembly, or convention. The
Tories of Queen's County, New York, were moved against by
direct action of the Congress by means of the continental army.

ing the establishment of a Form of Government, and Union with the United Colonies."[1]   And, finally, when the Congress was sufficiently strong to permit privateering, it adopted one of its most popular measures.   For, though the risks were great, the returns were so large as to interfere seriously with enlistments in the army—the pomp, and circumstance, and glory of war seemingly making weaker appeal to the patriots of those days, than the fortunes to be gained by the less poetic, but more remunerative preying upon England's commerce.

The carrying through of the resolutions outlined above was made possible only by the never-tiring aggressiveness of the radical minority, who made up for the slimness of their numbers by the stoutness of their intellects.   At the beginning of the year 1776 the outspoken advocates of independence then in the Congress were George Wythe of Virginia, Gadsen of South Carolina, McKean of Delaware, Franklin of Pennsylvania, Ward of Rhode Island, Deane of Connecticut, and Samuel Adams of Massachusetts.   The accession of the new Connecticut delegation, which arrived on January 16, followed by Samuel Chase, John Adams, and Elbridge Gerry shortly after, gave strength to their ranks, by way of ability, far in excess of their numbers. There were some losses as well, for Gadsen left

[1] *Journal of Congress,* March 20, 1776, Bradford edition.

about the middle of January to take part in the
affairs of his own colony, and Ward died on March
25. But the loss of the latter was more than made
good by the arrival of Richard Henry Lee, in the
second week of March. Until the end of April
they had no important additions to their numbers.
Upon the shoulders of these few men rested the
burden of the fight for independence in the Congress, and that it was carried on with such skill and
with ultimate success, was due to the inexhaustible
resourcefulness of their sharp wits. Largely
through their exertions the Congress had established
itself. For the next two months (May and June)
they bent their energies to forcing their way through
to their ultimate goal—a unanimous declaration of
independence.

But with all their aggressiveness and alertness
and ability, in spite of the great encouragement they
were giving to the popular party in Philadelphia,
and the pressure they could bring to bear on individual members, they had not been able to make
any impression on the Pennsylvania Assembly as a
whole. The local fight, now of several months
duration, to have that body agree to a material increase in the representation of the western counties
and of the city of Philadelphia, and to an extension
of the suffrage qualifications, proved almost barren
of result, except to incense further the popular party.

Yet the Assembly was so blind as not to see the extent and force of this popular uprising; and sitting in the room above that in which the Congress held its sessions, on the very day that the Congress was opening the ports of the country, the Assembly was obstinately voting, by a large majority, not to alter the instructions to the delegates on the subject of independence.[1]   But the Congress, grown somewhat arbitrary by the rapid advances toward independence it saw making elsewhere, would not sit idly by without taking some measure to show its sympathy with the disappointed democracy of Pennsylvania.   To the much dissatisfied elements in the western counties it had been responsive on a previous occasion,[2] as if to let the people there know that, though the Assembly was against them, the stronger arm of the Congress would be raised in their behalf whenever expedient.   The border warfare between the Pennsylvania and the Connecticut settlers at Wyoming still continued, and an opportunity arose in the middle of April for the Congress again to take a hand.[3]   It did this now with the more readiness, because it could thereby make known that the welfare of no part of the country was being overlooked, and that the inhabitants of

[1] See Lincoln, *op. cit.*, Chap. XIII.
[2] *Journal of Congress*, December 20, 1775.
[3] *Journal of Congress*, April 15, 1776.

the western counties in their dispute with the Pennsylvania Assembly would continue to find a sturdy
advocate before the Congress.

In the full flush of its new-found strength the
Congress went further afield and seeing, as it
thought, an opportunity to advance the interests of
the independence party in Maryland, proceeded
to attempt to lay down the rule of conduct for that
colony. The conditions were in some respects not
dissimilar from those in Pennsylvania, and the presence of a most amiable, respected, and popular governor, Eden, still exercising some of his functions,
served to complicate matters. He had been able, in
great measure, to keep control of the Convention and
Council of Safety, though the Baltimore Committee
had not proved so tractable. It was largely due to
his influence that Maryland had taken her stand
against independence, and though his authority was
waning at this time (the middle of April) it was as
yet far from gone. When, therefore, the Congress
had put before it, by the Baltimore Committee, a
batch of Eden's correspondence with the home authorities, it immediately responded by calling upon
the Maryland Council of Safety to seize and secure
the governor and have his papers relating " to the
American dispute, without delay conveyed safely to
Congress."[1] But the Congress had reckoned without its host.

[1] *Journal of Congress,* April 16, 1776.

Without delay, it is true, the Council of Safety took up the cause, but in a manner far different from what had been anticipated. Its members considered their dignity offended by the Congress acting at once upon the information provided by the Baltimore Committee, without first referring the matter to the Council of Safety. They denounced the Baltimore Committee, and especially its president, for exercising an authority which went far beyond the bounds to which it was considered they should have been limited, and the echoes of the controversy resounded in the halls of the Maryland Convention when it met a few weeks later.[1]   Instead of seizing Governor Eden, they considered his case for several weeks, and finally advised him to depart in peace with his possessions.[2]   When, therefore, the resolution of the Congress on the subject of forming new governments and putting an end to all authority derived from the crown,[3] came before them, they were still smarting under what they believed to be the insult put upon them by the Congress. Despite that they had less than a week before absolved all persons from taking the usual oaths to the government, upon assuming office, they now not only passed

[1] May 8, 1776, *Proc. of Md. Conventions*, Baltimore, 1836, 125.

[2] May 24, 1776, *Ibid.*, 150–152.

[3] See pp. 91–94.

long resolutions expressing their opinion that the
necessity had not yet arisen for suppressing the
exercise of every kind of authority under the crown,
and in its place having all the powers of government
exercised under the authority of the people, but went
further, and specifically notified the delegates in
the Congress to follow the old instructions directing
them not to vote for independence, " in the same
manner as if the said instructions were particularly
repeated."[1]   In this instance the intrusion of the
Congress into Maryland's affairs had retarded instead of advanced the cause of independence, and
the effects of the friction engendered between the
Congress and the Convention, and between Maryland's delegates and the President, Hancock, and
other delegates, did not wear off before six weeks
had passed away.

But a set-back of this nature did not daunt the
radicals, who were now finding popular support
throughout the colonies.   The measures that the
Congress had so far adopted were looked upon
everywhere as warranted by the necessities of the
situation.   From all sides information was coming
in that the popularity of independence was growing
apace.   The correspondence of the time, the
gazettes, the resolutions of local committees, all
were viewing with marked favor the idea that six

[1] *Proc. of Md. Conventions,* May 21, 142.

months before had found scarcely an advocate.[1]
These gave courage to the radicals in the Congress,
and furnished the incentive to pursue bolder measures still.   The inertia of the conservative middle
colonies had to be overcome, and if they would not
of themselves withdraw the instructions against
independence, the Congress would give them the
occasion.   This reasoning applied with particular
force to Pennsylvania, whose Assembly still stood
as a stone wall against all pressure brought to bear
on it, for as has been well said, " Pennsylvania was
the battle-ground of the movement at this time." [2]
Some direct appeal must be made which if not re-
plied to by the conservatives in a manner satisfactory to the independence party in Pennsylvania,
as elsewhere, would result in the overthrow of the
old order.

As if to provide the radicals with a lever with
which to raise out of their depths of doubt and hesi-
tation the many still hoping for commissioners or
other means of reconciliation, came the definite
news, early in May,[3] that great numbers of Han-
overian and Hessian soldiers were being sent over.
The cry against resorting to the aid of foreign mercenaries, who could have no interest in the contest,

[1] See Austin's *Gerry,* I, 179.
[2] John Adams' *Works,* III, 45, note.
[3] See p. 67.

and would, therefore, be certain to carry on the war with a cruelty not to be expected of those speaking their own language and having much in common with them, resounded through the land; and while serving to give pause to many who halted at the thought of the seeming impossibility of withstanding such an overwhelming force, aroused the spirit of a far greater number to meet the oncoming hosts with all the strength and determination within them.

John Adams, always ready for some bold stroke, now came forward and sought to force matters. He would have had the colonies that had put limitations upon the actions of their delegates, requested to repeal their instructions, giving as reason the present state of America and " the cruel efforts of our enemies " which rendered it necessary that a perfect union be formed to preserve and establish our liberties.[1]   But largely because of the feeling that prevailed in the minds of the more conservative that this was going too far for the time, and that the ultimate aim might be attained the better in another way, this motion in the form finally adopted was toned down considerably.   It made a recommendation to the assemblies and conventions, " where no government sufficient to the exigencies of their affairs hath been hitherto estab-

[1] Probably on May 6, 1776. See *Works,* II, 489.

lished, to adopt such government as shall in the opinion of the representatives of the people best conduce to the happiness and safety of their constituents in particular and America in general."[1] And this was followed by the selection of a radical committee to prepare a preamble intended to state the reason for advising such action.

In the interval between their appointment and the adoption of the preamble which they reported, two important incidents occurred, which could not have been without influence in shaping the course of the Congress' action. On the day before the final vote on the preamble was taken, Jefferson, fresh from his labors in Virginia, took his seat in the Congress, from which he had been absent for more than four months; and Ellery arrived from Rhode Island bringing with him new instructions, but just issued to her delegates by that colony, permitting them to vote for independence if joined by others.[2] Though Jefferson bore no new instructions, he was perfectly in touch with affairs in his own colony, knew how county upon county was demanding that the recently called convention should renounce allegiance to Great Britain, and was therefore ready to aid in every way in furthering such views. The Rhode Island in-

[1] *Journal of Congress,* May 10, 1776.
[2] These instructions are in *Journal of Congress,* May 14, 1776.

structions, though not mentioning independence (because in the phrasing of the astute governor of that colony, " dependency is a word of so equivocal a meaning, and hath been used to such ill purposes, and independency, with many honest and ignorant people carrying the idea of eternal warfare "),[1] were so general in their character as to give the delegation full powers to do or vote as they wished. With two such accessions to the ranks of the radicals in the Congress the preamble was carried through with a rush.

As usual, the occasion for giving the authority of the Congress to the recommendation now made to the colonies is sought in some British acts of aggression or shortcoming. These are stated to be the exclusion by the King, in conjunction with the Lords and Commons, of the colonies from the protection of his crown; the failure to answer the petition, and the use of the full force of the kingdom, combined with foreign mercenaries, to accomplish the subjugation of America. Under such circumstances " it appears absolutely unreconcilable to reason and good conscience, for the people of these colonies now to take the oaths and affirmations necessary for the support of any government under the crown of Great Britain." Instead, every kind of authority under the crown should be totally sup-

[1] Staples, *Rhode Island in the Continental Congress*, 68.

94 THE DECLARATION OF INDEPENDENCE

pressed, and all the powers of government exerted
by authority of the people of the colonies " for the
preservation of internal peace virtue and good order, as well as for the defence of their lives, liberties
and properties, against the hostile invasions and
cruel depredations of their enemies."[1]

To stay the passage of this preamble, to them more
offensive even than the resolution for which it furnished the pretext, Duane of New York, and Wilson
of Pennsylvania uttered loud and earnest protest.
They were fully cognizant that the intent of its
clauses was to compass the overthrow of the tottering Pennsylvania Assembly, and bring pressure to
bear upon the conservative elements of New York
and the other hesitating colonies. This could be done
only by an appeal to the people, and the Congress
had not dared as yet to go so far in proclaiming
its reliance upon them. But it was foreseen that
an appeal of another sort must shortly be made to
them to come forth in large numbers to fight the
greater future battles for liberty, compared with
which all the clashes that had already occurred were
as preliminary skirmishes. And to ensure the success
of its extensive plans the Congress was more than
willing to give the democracy, whenever it might,
some show to procure the rights which it was
clamoring for in louder and ever louder degree.

[1] *Journal of Congress,* May 15, 1776, Aitken edition, 1777.

Having been instrumental in accomplishing so much, John Adams could with good grace unbosom himself to his wife to this effect : " Great Britain has at last driven America to the last step, a complete separation from her ; a total absolute independence, not only of her Parliament, but of her Crown, for such is the amount of the resolve of the 15th, . . . This is effected by extinguishing all authority under the crown, Parliament, and nation, as the resolution for instituting governments has done, to all intents and purposes."[1]   In those few words John Adams touched upon the salient point of the resolution—the renouncement of the jurisdiction of the crown.   Hitherto this had not been brought seriously into question, in any of the public documents of the Congress.[2]   And the form this now took but foreshadowed the terms in which would be couched the definite Declaration of Independence itself.

The latter end of the month of May and the first week of June had crowded into these few days events, the bigness of which by far transcended anything that had gone before. The Congress was approaching rapidly to the highest point of its authority.   It had already assumed to give a committee full power, in carrying out its investigations,

[1] *Letters to his Wife*, I, 109–110.
[2] See Chapter VII.

to send for persons and papers.[1] This was an extension of jurisdiction that would not until now have been acquiesced in for a moment. The arrival on the twentieth of May of Button Gwinnett and Lyman Hall from Georgia, bringing with them broad instructions to agree to any of the acts of the Congress, was an important accession to the ranks of the radicals, even though these two represented few more than a handful of the revolutionists of Savannah. Thus strengthened, the Congress could, with the greater complacency, studiously ignore Maryland's reactionary resolutions, which were read in the Congress on the twenty-fourth.[2] Within a few days the consideration of plans for retrieving the miscarriages and blunders in Canada, and carrying on the war with determined energy was entered upon with enthusiasm. For this purpose Washington and Gates were called to the councils of the Congress from New York, where they were awaiting and preparing to meet the expected reinforcements to the British arms.

Under these circumstances, the instructions laid before the Congress by the North Carolina and Virginia delegates on May 27, proved welcome reading. North Carolina's provincial Congress had passed the resolution empowering her representa-

[1] *Journal of Congress,* May 8, 1776.
[2] See p. 89 *supra.*

tives to join with the delegates from the other colonies in declaring independence, on the twelfth of the month preceding. For some reason, not fully to be accounted for, its presentation had been thus long delayed. It was probably not sent off with promptness, and when received was held back by Hewes who, unaided, had born the brunt of guarding North Carolina's interests in Philadelphia, for several months past. Before presenting it he had thought well to wait a while in the hope that another delegate might arrive to share with him the heavy responsibility of taking so momentous a step. But no such considerations weighed with the Virginia delegation. Their instructions were more explicit than any hitherto passed. They were not merely to join with others in declaring independence when the Congress saw fit to adopt such a measure, but were to make the first move by presenting a specific proposal to that end. Only the multiplicity of affairs receiving consideration at this time, prevented the Congress from at once giving a hearing to Virginia's proposition.

The Congress was now on the point of making a call for greater numbers of troops than any hitherto sent out. Some attempt must be made to retrieve the miscarriages and disasters in Canada, and a bold front must be put on to meet the serious situation in New York.[1] To do this without stating

[1] *Journal of Congress*, June 1, 3, 1776.

7

publicly the reasons, so that all might be made familiar with them would arouse criticism, might even
cause dissension. To avoid this possibility, it was
decided to have the call for troops accompanied by a
stirring address that would " impress the minds of
the people with the necessity of now stepping forward to save their country, their freedom and property."[1] Moreover it was well understood that independence was now a question, at most, of only a
few weeks, and once declared, the Congress must
be in a position to sustain it by force of arms if need
be. For none appreciated better than the members
of the Congress, the necessity of being prepared to
suppress with determination the dissenters from the
measures for which it stood sponsor, from the day
when it renounced all connection with Great Britain.
The time was at hand when all must declare either
for the Congress or against it—and those who followed the latter course must be ready to pay the
full cost of their tenacity of opinion.

[1] *Secret Journal of Congress, Domestic,* May 29, 1776. The
address intended was never issued, as the Declaration of Independence more than took its place.

CHAPTER V

INDEPENDENCE IN THE MAKING

A brief survey of the status of the independence sentiment throughout the colonies at the opening of the month of June, as mirrored in the instructions to the delegates in the Congress, discloses the fact that but one colony, Virginia, had given unequivocal expression to its views. Excepting only that colony, none had directed that a definite proposal upon the subject of independence should be made; the five middle colonies had not rescinded their resolutions against it, and the instructions of only one other, North Carolina, mentioned the word. But throughout New England, the resolutions of the towns spoke as with one voice in favor of a declaration by the Congress. Massachusetts, carrying out her policy, laid down nearly two years before, had not officially come forward to demand what was the overwhelming desire of her inhabitants. She had made so many advances in the past, had seen so many of her grievances taken up and made common issue of, that she thought it well to let the great renouncement take its origin elsewhere. She would be content to show her mettle after the die was cast.

The middle colonies had not yet spoken; but they were in a ferment of discussion, and the day for deciding the all-important question could not long be put off. Of the southern colonies, the action of South Carolina alone was doubtful. The instructions to her delegates, issued by the revolutionary organization, which had overthrown the old form of government and substituted a new in its place, were comprehensive. But scarcely half a dozen of the men who were the leaders in the local revolutionary movement favored independence. The instructions could not, therefore, accurately be construed as authorizing a vote for independence. At most the delegates could use their best judgment as to the right course to follow.[1]

Such was the situation when on June 7, in accordance with the terms of Virginia's instructions, Richard Henry Lee, speaking for his colleagues, introduced the resolutions, written in his own hand and reading: "Resolved, That these United Colonies are, and of right ought to be, free and independent States, that they are absolved from all allegiance to the British Crown, and that all political connection between them and the State of Great Britain is, and ought to be, totally dissolved.

"That it is expedient to take the most effectual measures for forming foreign alliances.

[1] McCrady, *S. C. in the Revolution,* Chapter VI.

" That a plan of confederation be prepared and
transmitted to the respective Colonies for their consideration and approbation."[1]   That Virginia's delegation would propose the adoption of some such
statements, was foreseen ten days before when the
Congress had listened to the formal reading of the
resolves of the Virginia Convention. And if anything more were needed to strengthen the conviction
that it was useless to hope for a change of policy on
the part of Great Britain, and that Virginia's move
was, therefore, timely and appropriate, this was
furnished by the King's brief answer, just to hand,
delivered in reply to the address and petition of the
Lord Mayor and Aldermen of London on March
22.[2]   But even with the action of Virginia's delegation fully expected, and with the determined
words of the King before them, there must have
been something at least approaching a shock in Independence Chamber when this " hobgobling of so

[1] The original MS of these resolutions is among the Papers
of the Continental Congress recently transferred from the
Department of State to the Library of Congress.   The sheet
on which they are written has had added to it, partly in the
hand of Benjamin Harrison and partly in that of Charles
Thomson and another not identified, the determination of
Congress thereupon, as afterwards entered in the journal.
It also bears an endorsement in Thomson's hand. A facsimile
is in *Force,* 4th, VI, facing 1700.

[2] See *Force,* 4th, VI, 462–463.

frightful a mien "[1] actually stalked into their midst.
This may account for the unsatisfactory entry on
the *Journal of Congress,* which fails to inform us
who were the mover and seconder, though it duly
records that the resolutions obtained a second, and
from other sources we learn that it was John Adams
who thus spoke out.

For all that they had been long demanding action,
even the radicals entered upon the discussion of this
momentous subject not unmindful of the seriousness
of the consequences involved.   They were aggressive and persistent still, had advocated a reckless
course in times past, and were eager that a conclusion should be reached, but above all they perceived the necessity for unanimity, now more than
ever.   They were entirely willing, therefore, that
consideration should be postponed for a day, the
members being enjoined to attend punctually at ten
o'clock the next morning.   As if to foreshadow
the great part he was to play in fashioning the
document in which independence is proclaimed,
Jefferson, and he alone, made notes of the great
debates held on the eighth and tenth of June, and
on July 1.[2]   The main burden of the opposition fell
upon the shoulders of Wilson, Robert R. Livingston, Dickinson, and Edward Rutledge, all but the

[1] John Adams.
[2] *Works,* Ford edition, I, 18–28.

last representing the middle colonies. They held
that, though friendly to the measure, with them it
was a question of its opportuneness; there had
always been delay in taking any important step
until the voice of the people demanded it; the middle colonies were " not yet ripe for bidding adieu to
British connection, but they were fast ripening and
in a short time would join in the general voice of
America," and the dissensions created by the resolution of May 15, demonstrated this; that some delegations had not the authority to consent to such a
declaration, and certainly the delegates of the other
colonies had no power to answer for them; that
as the assembly of Pennsylvania, and the New York
convention were then in session, and conventions
would meet in Maryland, Pennsylvania, and New
Jersey in a few days, and would probably take up
the question of their attitude toward independence,
they should wait until they could be heard from;
that there was danger if such a declaration was
made now, the instructed delegates must retire, and
possibly their colonies might secede from the union.
Taking up the matter of foreign alliances, they
argued that it would be best to wait until they
learned from the agent sent to Paris as to the disposition of the French court; that by waiting, if the
ensuing campaign was successful, they could make
an alliance on better terms, and that they should

agree among themselves upon the terms on which
to form an alliance, before declaring to form one at
all events. It is probable, too, that some stress was
laid, at least by Dickinson, upon the desirability of
forming a confederation before declaring independence, as this was a point on which he is reported
to have laid particular emphasis during the preceding months.[1]

Against these contentions " the Power of all New
England, Virginia and Georgia " was thrown,[2]
though the principal spokesmen were John Adams,
Wythe, and Lee until his departure for Virginia on
June 10. They held that the arguments of the
opposition were not against the proposition itself
but its timeliness ; that the question was not one of
announcing something new, but by a declaration of
independence of announcing a fact which already

[1] Stillé's *Dickinson.* On July 21, 1775, Franklin brought
forward his plan of a confederation, which appears to have
been read in Congress but received no further consideration.
Secret Journal, Domestic, 283 *et seq.* A plan was considered
by the Congress, January 16, 1776 (*Diary of Richard Smith*),
but was opposed by Dickinson and Hooper among others.
This was probably a modification of Franklin's original plan,
which he had transmitted to various colonies for examination.
In all likelihood this was the plan published in the *Penna.
Evening Post,* for March 5, 1776, and it may have been published then in order to answer the objection that confederation should precede independence.

[2] Jefferson's *Works,* I, 19, note.

existed; they had never acknowledged the dominance of the people or Parliament of England, and
the restraints which they had imposed on trade,
derived effect only from acquiescence in them;
their allegiance to the King was now dissolved by
his assent to the late act of Parliament declaring
them out of his protection and by levying war upon
them; that James II had not formally declared the
English people out of his protection and " yet his
action proved it & the parliament declared it," and
this was their position.   They argued that the
prohibitory instructions, particularly of Pennsylvania, were drawn a long time back, when conditions were different; that the people were waiting
for the Congress to lead the way, and were in favor
of the measure though some of their representatives
were not. Attacking the " proprietary powers "
(in which we hear the voice of John Adams) as
responsible for this backward attitude of Pennsylvania and Maryland, they held that the conduct of
some colonies from the beginning gave rise to the
suspicion that it was their policy to lag behind the
rest in order that " their particular prospect might
be better, even in the worst event," that the colonies
which had come forward in the beginning and
hazarded all must do so now, and " put all again
to their own hazard."   As to secession, they had
no fears, and even if the dissatisfied colonies seceded

(and here again the sound of John Adams's voice is unmistakable) " the history of the Dutch revolution proved that a secession of some colonists would not be so dangerous as some apprehended." Respecting foreign alliances, no nation of Europe would treat with us or receive an ambassador from us unless we were first independent, that they might not even afterward, but we should never know without trying; that the ensuing campaign might prove unsuccessful, and that an alliance had better be proposed " while our affairs wear a hopeful aspect."

It becomes clear from an examination of these debates, (which took place in committee of the whole with Harrison of Virginia in the chair), even in the fragmentary form in which they have come down to us, that all energies had to be concentrated on the middle colonies if they were to be won over to acquiesce in the determination reached by the seven other colonies, and that the opposing conventions and assemblies must be informed of the attitude of the majority of the Congress. A compromise involving delay was, therefore, a welcome proposal. So that when Edward Rutledge, on behalf of his colony, moved on the tenth that the consideration of the first resolution be postponed for three weeks, it was passed with the proviso that in order that no time might be lost in case the Congress finally agreed thereto, a committee should be selected to prepare a declaration which should serve as a preamble to the resolution.[1]   On the next day Jefferson, John Adams, Franklin, Sherman, and R. R. Livingston were chosen as the committee to have charge of preparing this important document.   And in the hope of influencing Dickinson and Morris, who contended for the making of foreign alliances and a confederation in advance of declaring independence, committees to prepare a plan of treaties to be proposed to foreign powers, and to draft articles of confederation, were selected on the twelfth.   Significant of the great awakening in the Congress that these debates occasioned, as of the necessity for a more orderly conduct of military affairs, which passing events disclosed, is the institution on this same day of the most important permanent organization within the Congress, the board of war and ordnance—a proposal for the creation of which had laid on the desk unacted upon for nearly two months.[2]

Turning now to what was happening in the middle colonies, we discover everywhere discussion of and action on the great question.   The resolution of the Congress of May 15 had proved, as was intended, of immediate effect in Philadelphia in spurring on the elements dissatisfied with the unchanged

[1] *Journal of Congress,* June 10, 1776.
[2] The Committee on establishing a War Office had reported on April 18, *Journal of Congress.*

attitude of the Pennsylvania Assembly. On the
twentieth of that month a general gathering of the
inhabitants of the City and Liberties, to the number, it is said, of 7,000, presided over by one of the
most disgruntled and influential of the radicals,
Col. Daniel Roberdeau, protested against the Assembly's competency to form a new government, and
resolved that a convention should be chosen by the
people for that purpose.[1]   These resolutions were
sent out to the committees of the counties of the
province, and June 18 was named as the day
on which a provincial conference should meet
in Philadelphia to determine upon the method of
electing members to a convention to establish the new
form of government, recommended by the Continental Congress.   The tottering Assembly in the
meantime was having difficulty in getting a quorum
together, though this was finally obtained on May
22.   They did little more for the next few days
than listen to elaborate addresses presented by the
radical and conservative inhabitants respectively, the
one demanding that no action be taken upon the
resolution of the Congress of May 15, and the other
that the old instructions to the delegates against independence be adhered to.   On the fifth of June
they listened to the reading of Virginia's resolutions transmitted by the convention of that colony,

[1] Lincoln, *Revolutionary Movement in Pennsylvania*, 255.

and, by a large majority, decided to appoint a committee, with Dickinson as chairman, to prepare new
instructions to the delegates in the Congress. These
were adopted on the eighth, but not signed by the
speaker until the day, June 14, on which the old
Assembly passed forever out of existence, by reason
of the impossibility of reconciling the conservative
spirit of its members with the revolutionary ideas
prevailing among large numbers of the people, who
had taken affairs into their own hands. The instructions tried to effect a compromise when the
time for compromises was long past, and consequently displeased the conservatives who thought
they went too far, and were unsatisfactory to the
radicals, because they did not go far enough. While
specifically authorizing the delegates to enter into
a confederation and to make treaties with foreign
powers, they dodged the main issue, independence,
by merely bestowing the power to concur in adopting such other measures as were judged necessary.
In such a crisis plain speaking was required, and no
resort to subterfuges would answer. Accordingly,
when the Conference of Committees came together
on the eighteenth of June, under the presidency of the
active Thomas McKean, a member of the Congress,
though having no power to instruct the delegates,
they unanimously expressed the willingness to concur in a vote of the Congress declaring the colonies

free and independent states.[1]   Thus ended the
struggle for authority to declare independence in
Pennsylvania, as a result of which the colony was
so rent asunder that it took many years to recover
from the effects.

We miss from this record the familiar name of
Franklin, who throughout the first six months had
been as much the leader of the radicals as Dickinson
of the moderates.   He was not now holding aloof
from choice, but fallen a victim to the racking
twinges of the gout, was kept from " Congress &
Company " for nearly all of the first three weeks of
June.   If the void left by his absence could have
been filled, Thomas McKean was at hand for this.
Not content with taking a leading part in fashioning Pennsylvania's affairs, he went through the
counties of Delaware and by his personal exertions
swung her into line for independence on June 14,[2]
the wording of the Philadelphia conference, with
which he had so much to do, being used.   It must be
remembered, when we wonder how a Pennsylvanian
could have been permitted to interfere in Delaware,
that Pennsylvania men and measures were not then
so separated from Delaware's politics as now.

Some measure of the extent of the changes
wrought in New Jersey by the revolution, is revealed

[1] *Force,* 4th, VI, 963.
[2] *Life and Correspondence of George Read,* 165 ; *Force,* 4th,
VI, 884 ; Frothingham's *Rise of the Republic,* 523.

by the fact that of the men who met in Provincial
Congress at Burlington on June 10, but six had
been members of the assembly of that colony which
had met for the last time in November of the previous year.   There as in Maryland, matters were
complicated by the presence of a popular governor,
William Franklin, who, though out of touch with
the Provincial Congress, still had the support of a
large body of the population.   To deprive him of
further influence to delay agreement upon independence it was thought best to get him out of the
colony, but he and his party were so strong that the
Provincial Congress were not willing to undertake
his banishment without the authority and assistance
of the Continental Congress, as " the countenance
and approbation of the Continental Congress would
satisfy some persons who might otherwise be disposed to blame " them.[1]   The Congress, on the lookout for a chance to shape the course of events, especially in a colony that had not yet rescinded its
old instructions against independence, responded immediately upon the receipt of this appeal.   Directing the examination of the governor, if as a result
it was decided that he should be confined, the
Congress stood ready to name the place, " they con-
curring in the sentiment . . . that it would be

[1] Letter of the New Jersey Congress to Continental Congress,
June 18, 1776, *Force,* 4th, VI, 1624.

improper to confine him in that colony." Before another week went round, Governor Franklin was ordered, by the Congress, to be sent to Connecticut.[1] Four days after New Jersey's first appeal, the Provincial Congress—having, one June 21, declared itself in favor of forming a new government pursuant to the recommendation of the Congress— voted new instructions to the delegates in the Congress, by which they were authorized to join in declaring independence, in making a confederation, and in contracting foreign alliances. In all this the hand of Jonathan D. Sergeant is visible. He, like McKean, was also a member of the Congress and knew well the temper of the majority of that body, though he had not for some weeks been in his place in Independence Chamber. His personality looms almost as large in the events that brought about the adhesion of New Jersey to the new doctrine, as McKean's in Pennsylvania and Delaware, Jay's in New York, and Chase's in Maryland.

Chase returned from the mission he was sent on to Canada too late by one day to take part in the debates held in the Congress. But this enforced silence served to make his pen all the more active when he learned how necessary it was for the cause of independence, to turn Maryland about. The Convention of that colony had adjourned on May 25, in angry

[1] *Journal of Congress,* June 19, 24, 1776.

mood at the Congress for its interference in her affairs, and was not to reassemble until the following August. But the requisitions for troops, made by the Congress, rendered it necessary for the Council of Safety to call the Convention to meet at Annapolis on June 21. That same day they instructed their deputies in Philadelphia to ask for leave of absence to attend the Convention, and at the same time to make an agreement to postpone consideration of the questions of independence, foreign alliances and confederation until their return.[1] The Congress, however, would not listen to any proposal for deferring the vote, as it was public property that this would take place on July 1, and the country was expectant.[2] Meantime, Chase, as he put it, had " not been idle." He had appealed in writing to every county committee, and one after the other they were directing their representatives in the Convention to vote for new instructions to the delegates in the Congress. And in winning over the members of the Convention to his way of thinking he received able support from Charles Carroll, of Carrollton, his companion on the mission to Canada. Just a week after the Convention met, the fruit of their toil was manifested in the unanimous resolve, passed late at night, directing Maryland's delegates

[1] *Proc. Md. Conventions*, 166.
[2] John Adams' *Works*, IX, 413.

8

to join with the other colonies in voting in favor of independence.[1]   Immediately after this decision was reached, Chase wrote to John Adams, in triumph: " I am this moment from the House to procure an Express to follow the Post with an Unan: vote of our Convention for *Independence* etc. etc.—see the glorious effects of County Instructions—our people have fire if not smothered."[2]   Without his opportune exertions it is safe to say that Maryland would have lagged behind many weeks longer.

Excepting only New York, each of the middle colonies, spurred on by the persistent agitation of some member of the Congress, before the month was out, in one way or another had given to its delegates the authority that was so much desired, and which was all important, if independence was to be proclaimed as the unanimous act of the colonies. As for the remainder of the country there was doubt about only one other colony, South Carolina. For in response to the repeated demands of their delegates, Connecticut and New Hampshire had taken action on June 14 and 15 respectively[3]   And, though the assemblies of Massachusetts and Rhode Island[4] had not instructed in precise terms, the

---

[1] *Proc. Md. Conventions,* 176.
[2] John Adams' *Works,* III, 56.
[3] *Force,* 4th, VI, 868, 1030.
[4] See p. 92 *supra.*

voice of the people within their borders was calling so loudly for the proclaiming of independence, that none could have any doubt how the votes of their representatives would be cast. All knew, also, how stood Virginia, North Carolina, and Georgia. But a question in the minds of many as the fateful day approached, was "How would South Carolina and New York decide?" No more definite word had issued from the former than that spoken more than three months before, when her delegates were empowered to join with a majority of the other colonies in executing such measures as would promote the best interests of that colony in particular, and America in general. None familiar with the political situation in South Carolina at the time these instructions were passed by her Provincial Congress can, in fairness, construe them as an authorization to vote for independence.[1] But in the three months interval the aggressive, efficient, local minority favoring independence had been as active in beating down the opposition (or at least in gaining control of the administrative machinery), as had been that other minority, with success so marked, in the Continental Congress. If her instructions had not been rendered more explicit, the conditions had certainly undergone a change, and it was for South Carolina's

[1] See McCrady, *South Carolina in the Revolution.* Also p. 100 *supra.*

delegates in the Congress to determine whether these were so altered as to serve as warrant for joining their vote to that of the majority.

New York, much divided in her counsels by local political and religious dissensions of long standing, as by the presence of a large body of Tory sympathizers, the effects of which had colored all her acts in the past, had shown as yet no inclination to make haste in reaching a decision. It would well repay us to go into the history of the complex conditions in that colony, but we would thereby be carried too far afield.[1] And, though there was anxious waiting to hear what would be her attitude, it must be remembered that she occupied not nearly so large nor so critical a place as Pennsylvania, nor wielded so much influence. Therefore, after it was known how Pennsylvania would in all probability vote, New York's position was not so important in the councils of the Congress, so far as independence was concerned, as it would have been had there still been doubt of Pennsylvania. Reliance, too, was placed upon the influence that the large increases in the army soon to be gathered about New York, would have in shaping opinion in favor of the

[1] For the details of New York's complex political affairs see Flick, *Loyalism in New York, passim,* Van Tyne's *Loyalists in the Am. Rev.,* Chapter V, and for the earlier period, Dr. Becker's valuable studies in *Am. Hist. Rev.* and *Pol. Sci. Quarterly.*

Congress's decrees.   Suffice it, therefore, for our purposes to record that on May 31 resolutions were passed by her Provincial Congress respecting the recommendation of the Congress of May 15.   They were to the effect that having doubts as to the authority of the Provincial Congress to deal with so important a subject as instituting a new form of government, the people were to be given the opportunity of determining this matter.   The electors in the several counties of the colony were recommended to hold a special election of deputies (in the manner and form prescribed for the election of the existing Congress) to a Congress that should meet in New York on the second Monday in July. The deputies thus elected were to be understood as being thereby authorized to form a new government if they deemed it wise, which was " to continue in force until a future peace with Great Britain shall render the same unnecessary."[1]   There was nothing in this that could seriously offend the sensibilities of those still conservatively inclined, for in spite of the declaration that the people should determine the question, the ultimate decision was left in the hands of the Provincial Congress.

Immediately after the vote in the Continental Congress on independence, on June 8, four of the New York delegates then in Philadelphia, sent an

[1] *Force,* 4th, VI, 1352.

express to their Provincial Congress telling them
that a vote on independence could be expected to
be had soon and asking for instructions. Three
days later the Provincial Congress passed resolutions recommending the electors and freeholders
to instruct the representatives, for whom they were
to vote at the ensuing election, respecting the attitude they should hold on the question of independence. But at the same time, with striking inconsistency, they voted not to publish these resolutions
until after the election had taken place.[1] Desiring
to explain this paradoxical action to the delegates
at Philadelphia, the letter in which the information
was conveyed served only to confuse them the more.
They were told that the Provincial Congress was
unanimously of the opinion that the instructions
did not authorize them " to give the sense of this
colony on the question of declaring it to be, and
continue, an independent state,"—a fact that was
so well understood by the delegates as not to need
affirmation by the unanimous opinion of the Provincial Congress. Further, they said they did not
feel inclined to instruct on that point, as the
majority held they had no authority so to do;
and they were fearful to ask the opinion of the
people at that time, lest it might interfere with the
elections that were to determine the question of a

[1] *Force,* 4th, VI, 1396.

new form of government.[1] In plain words, they wanted to insure their own reëlection to power, did not want to take any steps that might put this result in jeopardy, nor add to the numerous complications that already had arisen, and had, therefore, decided to postpone action on independence until the new convention met. The perplexed delegates in Philadelphia were thus left suspended in mid-air. And to add to their difficulties, they had doubts how to vote after independence was declared, when measures, the outcome of such action, were up for consideration.[2] In the meantime, the approach of the British army to New York caused the Provincial Congress to adjourn, on June 30, to meet at White Plains on July 8, so that at this crucial period, the delegates in Philadelphia were left without an authority to whom they might appeal for directions, until the vote on independence had taken place. On the tenth of July the deputies, just elected under the terms of the resolution of May 31, met at White Plains, resolved themselves into a convention and listened to the reading of the Declaration of Independence. The question of taking some stand was thus forced upon them, and a committee with Jay as chairman was selected to suggest suitable action. Since the discovery of Tryon's plot against

[1] *Force*, 4th, VI, 814.
[2] *Ibid.*, 1212.

Washington a considerable change of opinion had
come over enough of the members to form a majority, and they saw that only radical measures
could counteract the influence of the Tories, and
the presence of the British army.   Therefore,
on the afternoon of the same day they reported
resolutions, which were unanimously adopted, approving the declaration of the Continental Congress and pledging themselves to support it; the
final act being played on July 15, when these resolutions were read before the Continental Congress,
thereby rendering it possible to give the engrossed
copy the title of " The unanimous Declaration of
the thirteen united States of America."

CHAPTER VI

ADOPTING AND SIGNING THE DECLARATION

While the colonies were thus preparing for the final day, the committee, to whom had been entrusted the difficult and exacting task of framing a declaration suitable to serve as introductory to and in justification of the resolution of independence, had concluded its work. On Friday, the twenty-eighth of June, the document in Jefferson's handwriting, after being read before the Congress, was laid on the table. Had Jefferson alone, without opportunity to consult his associates, received the mandate of the Congress to draw up such a paper, it would have differed in no essential detail from that handed in. For not only was it the product of his pen, but it bears the stamp of his master mind in every phrase. At the first meeting of the committee he had been requested to undertake the preparation of the document. Upon its completion he submitted it separately to Adams and Franklin, who made only a few verbal alterations, and it was then reported to the full committee. Sherman and Livingston apparently performed no service beyond lending their approval.[1] As chairman of the committee it was

[1] I have followed Jefferson's account (*Works*, I, 24–27) as the only nearly contemporary version. It is but fair to add,

Jefferson's right to draw up the report, and his colleagues' request overcame any reluctance he may
have had to enter upon so important an undertaking.

The last two days of June happened to fall on
Saturday and Sunday. As the Congress had decided
a short time before, to hold no sessions on these days,
in order that the hard pressed committees might have
some leisure in which to consult upon the work given
over to them, consideration of the Declaration went
over until the next session, on July 1. At nine
o'clock the Congress met, and, as if these events had
been predesigned to render the day more solemn
still, it heard from New Jersey's Convention that
Howe was at Sandy Hook, and that some fifty British sail of the line had been sighted; and learned
from Washington of the unearthing of a serious con-
spiracy instigated by the Mayor of New York and
Governor Tryon. With his accustomed reserve,
Washington intimated by no word that the danger
to himself was of any consequence, though we may
gather from other sources that nothing short of his
own assassination was aimed at. But some slight relief was obtained from reflecting upon such de-

however, that Adams in his autobiography, written many years
later, differs as to details. Naturally, as a result of the
greater clamor that by that time surrounded the Declaration,
he exaggerated the part he had played in its preparation. See
Works of John Adams, III, 512 *et seq.*

pressing intelligence, when the welcome resolution of Maryland's Convention was made known to all, disclosing that another vote was sure to be added to the majority favoring independence.[1]

After reading the order of the day, the consideration of the resolution upon independence was proceeded with in committee of the whole, with Harrison of Virginia in the chair. The Declaration was referred to this committee also, but was not under discussion until the following day, July 2, when the resolution had been disposed of. As Hancock was the permanent president of the Congress, so Harrison may be regarded as its permanent chairman of the committee of the whole. He had served in that capacity for many months, the Congress by this means aiming to restore to Virginia her weight of prominence in the colonial balance, that had been lost to Massachusetts by Hancock's election to the presidency. Great debates were on once again, and for the final time, and engrossed the attention of the Congress for the entire day (July 1). Relying as we must, upon accounts written many years afterward, when memories proved treacherous, it would appear, nevertheless, that John Adams and John Dickinson again stepped forth as principal champions for and against the adoption of Lee's resolution declaring independence.

[1] *Journal of Congress,* July 1, 1776. See p. 113 *supra.*

John Adams tells us that he made his speech for
the benefit and at the desire of the newly arrived
New Jersey delegates, who had not been present on
the seventh and eighth of June, and had therefore
missed the earlier debates.[1] But of the words he
then uttered no trace remains. In these circumstances we can only state that he recapitulated arguments made " twenty times before," all of which, he
thought, was " an idle misspence of time, for nothing was said but what had been repeated and hackneyed in that room before, a hundred times for six
months past."[2] That he delivered a speech, however, of unusual force and brilliancy is certain, and
that it had considerable influence upon the minds of
some who still were undecided how to act, is quite
beyond doubt.

For the precise contribution of Dickinson on this
important occasion, we are equally at a loss. But
if there is no record of his words, we have by way
of substitute the opinions he held at that time, set
down by his own hand six years and a half later,
which Bancroft has taken the liberty of dressing up
to give them the appearance of the speech he is
known to have delivered. Dickinson would have us
believe that his opposition was based on the inadvisability of issuing a declaration of independence

[1] *Works*, III, 58.
[2] *Ibid.*, IX, 415.

at that time. " The right and authority of Congress
to make it, the justice of making it I acknowledged.
The policy of *then* making it I disputed." He would
have had the Congress await the result of some decisive battle, upon which, and not upon the Declaration, would depend procuring foreign aid; and he
believed that " the formation of our governments,
and an agreement upon the terms of our confederation, ought to precede the assumption of our station
among sovereigns." To his mind the logical order
was, first, the creation of local governments, to be
followed by a confederation, and then independence.
The importance of a confederation rested on the
security it would give to the weaker colonies, against
the dangers of having disadvantageous terms imposed on them by the stronger. These are the main
points on which he based his arguments, as contained
in the elaborate vindication of his career contributed,
appropriately enough, to Freeman's Journal in 1783.[1]

It is altogether probable that others participated
in the discussion on this day, for the sitting was
protracted until late in the afternoon, but we have
no authentic statements of anything that was said.
The debate having run its course, and the vote being
taken, it was discovered that all New England, New
Jersey, Maryland, Virginia, North Carolina, and

[1] This *Vindication* is to be found in Stillé's *Dickinson,* Appendix V.

Georgia favored the resolution, and South Carolina and Pennsylvania voted against it. Delaware's ballot went for naught, since McKean favored and George Read opposed it, and New York's delegates decided that the only course they could pursue was to refrain from voting. Nine colonies thus registered themselves as willing to cast off the yoke, an overwhelming majority to be sure, yet far from the unanimity which had been hoped for and worked for. As soon as Harrison, in his capacity of chairman of the committee of the whole, reported the decision to the Congress, Edward Rutledge of South Carolina again exercised the privilege of having the final determination postponed, which he had made use of on June 10. The members, however, were now so eager to conclude the consideration of this momentous subject that delay was voted but for a day.

The position of the South Carolina delegates was extremely embarrassing. That a majority of them, under Rutledge's guidance, favored independence, there can be no question. The issue now before them, however, was not that of giving expression to individual opinion, but of casting the vote of the colony of South Carolina as the majority of her people would have desired. If the view of the most recent historian of that state be correct, there was not only a decided opposition to inde-

pendence in that colony, but there was nothing in
the history of the relations between South Carolina
and the home government to create a sentiment in
its favor.[1]   On the other hand, the South Carolina
delegates in the Congress were confronted with the
probability that when the final vote was taken no
colony, unless it be their own, would be found voting in the negative.   They were naturally reluctant
to incur the responsibility of thus marking theirs as
the only colony to stand in the way of practical
unanimity.   Therefore they took ready advantage
of the opportunity for another day's delay, which
the rules allowed.   It would appear that Rutledge
was the most forward among them and the boldest,
that he bent the others to his will, and made them
willing to cast in their lot with the rest and brave
the consequences at home.   Fortunately for them,
we are told, " a battle had been fought, a British
fleet had been repulsed, a British army held in check,
and a victory won in Charlestown harbor, before the
news of their action in Congress," was known
among their fellows.   All this changed the condition of parties and affairs, and gave welcome reception to the intelligence of the part the delegates had
played in the drama at Philadelphia.[2]

During the day's interval, McKean of Delaware

[1] McCrady, *S. C. in the Revolution,* 172.
[2] *Ibid.,* 173–174.

had been active in his endeavor to get an additional delegate from his colony to counterbalance George Read's opposition. He tells us that he sent an express-rider at his own expense for Caesar Rodney to Dover. Riding the eighty miles at post-haste, Rodney was met by McKean at the State House door and brought into Congress in his boots, just before the vote was taken.[1] At least three of Pennsylvania's delegates, Dickinson, Morris, and Wilson, were in as sore perplexity as those of South Carolina. Bearing credentials from the Pennsylvania Assembly, they had seen its authority diminish gradually, until a quorum could no longer be obtained, and it had now passed out of existence. In its stead a revolutionary organization, with which they had no sympathy, had assumed control of Pennsylvania's affairs. The Conference of Committees, just organizing into a convention to prepare a form of government, had given authority to vote for independence, but to Wilson, Dickinson, and Morris, this Conference had not itself the authority which it was conferring upon others. On the other hand, as far-seeing men, it was plain to them that the old order was overturned, its vitality gone, with little likelihood of its revival. Under these circumstances, but one of them, Wilson, rose to the occasion. As Dickinson and Morris stayed away from

[1] Buchanan's *McKean Family*.

the Congress when the vote was taken, Wilson decided to go with the majority. His decision was all-important, for without his vote Pennsylvania's delegation would have been equally divided and her vote would have gone for naught. Dickinson in spite of his services in the field did not for many years recover the prestige which he lost at this time. Robert Morris, notwithstanding that he was in opposition to the popular desires, is the only member who was returned to the Congress. He was thus given the opportunity to serve his state and his country in so signal a manner in after years, as almost to obliterate all memory of his antagonism to independence.[1]

Thus, when the final vote was taken on the resolution on the morning of July 2, but three votes, so far as we know, were cast against it—those of Willing and Humphreys of Pennsylvania, and Read's of Delaware. But Wilson, Franklin, and Morton outvoted Willing and Humphreys, and McKean and Rodney set Read's opposition at naught. All the other colonies, excepting only New York, whose delegates abstained from taking part, voted without a dissenting voice for the resolution.

This out of the way, the Congress now for the first time undertook to consider, in committee of the

[1] See, for Morris's own statement of his views, his letter to Joseph Reed, July 20, 1776, Reed's *Reed*, I, 201.

whole, Jefferson's Declaration which was to serve as justification for the resolution just adopted. For the remainder of that day and most of the next two, beginning at the early hour of nine o'clock, this the most picturesque and interesting of all of America's state documents was under consideration, paragraph by paragraph, what time the flying camp was ordered out both to protect New Jersey and stand ready to Washington's call, and rations of rum were being voted to shipwrights on Lake Champlain. The principal changes resolved upon by reason of this discussion are thus described by Jefferson: " The pusillanimous idea that we had friends in England worth making terms with, still haunted the minds of many. For this reason those passages which conveyed censures on the people of England were struck out, lest they should give them offence. The clause, too, reprobating the enslaving the inhabitants of Africa, was struck out in complaisance to South Carolina and Georgia, who had never attempted to restrain the importation of slaves, and who on the contrary still wished to continue it. Our Northern brethren also I believe felt a little tender under these censures; for though their people have very few slaves themselves, yet they had been pretty considerable carriers of them to others."[1]

The first of the paragraphs he had in mind when

[1] *Works,* I, 28.

penning these words, reads: " and when occasions
have been given them, by the regular course of their
laws, of removing from their councils the disturbers
of our harmony, they have by their free election re-
established them in power. At this very time too
they are permitting their chief magistrate to send
over not only soldiers of our common blood, but
Scotch and foreign mercenaries to invade and destroy us. These facts have given the last stab to
agonizing affection, and manly spirit bids us to renounce forever these unfeeling brethren. We must
endeavor to forget our former love for them, and
hold them as we hold the rest of mankind, enemies
in war, in peace friends. We might have been a free
and a great people together; but a communication of
grandeur and of freedom it seems is below their
dignity. Be it so since they will have it. The road
to happiness and to glory is open to us too, we will
tread it apart from them. . . . " These sentences
were intended to be inserted in the paragraph just
before that beginning " We, therefore, the Representatives," and were to follow the sentence, " They
too have been deaf to the voice of justice and of consanguinity." Their excision displays no pusillan-
imity, as Jefferson would have it, but rather a better
appreciation of the necessity for the retention of
essentials and the discarding of dispensable details.

The other paragraph had reference to the slave-
trade and was more denunciatory of the King than
any of the remainder. It read : " he has waged cruel
war against human nature itself, violating its most
sacred rights of life and liberty in the persons of a
distant people who never offended him, captivating
and carrying them into slavery in another hemisphere, or to incur miserable death in their transportation thither. This piratical warfare, the opprobrium of *infidel* powers, is the warfare of this
CHRISTIAN king of Great Britain determined to
keep open a market where MEN should be bought
and sold. He has prostituted his negative for suppressing every legislative attempt to prohibit or restrain this execrable commerce. And that this assemblage of horrors might want no fact of distinguished die, he is now exciting those very people to
rise in arms among us, and to purchase that liberty
of which *he* has deprived them, by murdering the
people upon whom he also obtruded them : thus paying off former crimes committed against the *liberties*
of one people, with crimes which he urges them to
commit against the *lives* of another." This is unquestionably one of the most forcible clauses that
issued from Jefferson's pen, and its rejection, for the
reasons which he ascribes, served to promote consistency of action on the part of the colonies, and
prevent the forcing of an issue which the country

was not yet in a position to face. But its omission was a serious blow to Jefferson, who all his days was a firm advocate of the suppression of the slave trade and of slavery.

The remaining changes that the Declaration underwent, were for the most part verbal and slight, and all tended in the direction of greater precision and terseness of expression. Thus concluded in committee of the whole on the afternoon of the fourth, it was reported to the Congress by Harrison, was read again, and received the final sanction of the Congress as the justification for the act that established a new nation among the powers of the world.

But[1] three of the many state documents that issued from the Continental Congress, during the nearly fifteen years of its existence, were regarded as of sufficient importance to have the signatures of the members appended: the Articles of Association, the Declaration of Independence, and the Articles of Confederation. Together they form the fundamental acts of union previous to the Constitution. The first two were of the nature of pledges on the part of the colonies to support one another in the

[1] Much information has been derived in the preparation of the following pages, from Judge Mellen Chamberlain's essay on the *Authentication of the Declaration of Independence* in the volume, "John Adams, etc.", Boston, 1898. But the results have been arrived at by independent researches as well.

fight against the common enemy, and the last was designed to be an instrument by which the federal relations of the states were to be regulated. Respecting the dates on which the Association and the Confederation were signed no question has ever been raised. It is to be regretted that the same statement does not hold regarding the Declaration of Independence. Ever rising in picturesque importance as the most familiar, and perhaps the most significant of the acts of the time, a wealth of tradition has grown up about its signing and promulgation. Unfortunately much of this is false and meaningless, notably that which connects the so-called Liberty Bell with the events of the day.[1] For the diffusion of the popular misconception respecting the signing there is ample warrant, in that the two principal sources of information which should be authoritative, are misleading.

[1] With the rehabilitation by which Independence Hall profited from the Centennial year, went the elevation of the bell to the position of unwarranted prominence which has since that time become more marked still. There is no shadow of authority even for associating the ringing of the bell with the announcement of the agreement upon independence. The mythical legend of the blue-eyed boy waiting outside the door to give the signal to the man in the bell tower is the product of the fertile imagination of one of Philadelphia's early romancers, George Lippard, who first gave currency to it in his appropriately called "Legends of the Revolution,— The 4th of July, 1776," 391 *et seq.*

They are an incorrectly printed journal of the proceedings of the Congress, and a carelessly composed
heading to the engrossed document.

To understand how the errors crept in and what
they signify, it is necessary to have before us the
paragraphs of the printed Journal. And it must also
be borne in mind that the proceedings of the Congress for the year 1776 were first printed, by order
of the Congress, by Robert Aitken, in the spring of
1777. After recording that the Declaration had
been agreed to in committee of the whole, and was
reported to the Congress, this sentence occurs in the
Journal for July 4: "The declaration being read
was agreed to as follows." The declaration is then
printed in its proper place, but in larger type than
that used for the remainder of the entries. After its
conclusion and in the ordinary type, we find the sentence, "The foregoing declaration was by order of
Congress engrossed and signed by the following
members," followed by fifty-five names, headed by
Hancock's, the remainder being arranged in single
column,[1] in geographical order beginning with New
Hampshire and ending with Georgia. This entry
has been the occasion of most of the confusion of
subsequent years. Though the statement is not made

[1] This is the arrangement in the Aitken edition of the Journal, Philadelphia, 1777. In some of the later editions the
signatures were in double columns.

that the members signed on the date under which
their names are entered, and it is a well-known fact
that more than a fourth of the members whose names
appear were not present on that day, some of them
not even being members at that time, none the less
the fact that the names appear with the proceedings
of July 4, has caused the popular error to creep in
which couples the signing and the adoption of the
document as events of the same date.

For a full elucidation of this matter, it is necessary to reproduce the subsequent entries bearing
upon the signing and official promulgation of the
document. On the same day (July 4) the printed
Journal informs us that a resolution was adopted
to send copies of the document to the several assemblies, conventions, and committees or councils of
safety, to the commanding officers of the continental
troops; and to have it proclaimed in each of the
United States[1] and at the head of the army. On
the 19th, four days after it was made known to the
Congress that New York had given her tardy assent to the wishes of the remainder, it was determined to have the Declaration " passed on the 4th,
. . . fairly engrossed on parchment, with the title
and style of ' The Unanimous Declaration of the
Thirteen United States of America '; and that the

[1] This is the first use of the phrase " United States " after
the Declaration.

same, when engrossed, be signed by every member
of Congress." On the second of August the Journal records that " The Declaration of Independence,
being engrossed, and compared at the table, was
signed by the members." These last two entries
appear in print only in the Secret Journal, first published in 1821, as if it was the intention thereby to
protect for a time the members who subscribed their
names to an act that would have rendered them
liable to trial for treason, if the revolution had been
suppressed by the British government. And, further, the first official reference to signing the Declaration, coming as it does two weeks after its
adoption, would seem to indicate, also, that the idea
of thus consummating the act was an afterthought.
On the 8th of January of the following year,
when the approach of the British to Philadelphia had rendered it necessary to transfer temporarily the scene of activities to Baltimore, the
Congress agreed for the first time to have an authentic copy of the Declaration printed with the
names of the members who had subscribed it, and
to send one to each of the states with the request " to have the same put upon record."[1] The

[1] This was the first issue of the Declaration giving the
names of the signers. It was printed at " Baltimore in Maryland, by Mary Katharine Goddard." Copies of this broadside
are very rare, the only k..own copies being in the New York
Public Library (Lenox), the Boston Public Library, and
among the archives of the state of Massachusetts, cxlii, 23.

records as reproduced above are the only references
to the Declaration in the printed Journal subsequent
to July 4.

Turning now to the original manuscripts, we find
in the entry for July 4 a significant disagreement
with the printed Journal. In the first place there
are two manuscript Journals among the volumes of
the Continental Congress papers, now deposited in
the Library of Congress, covering the proceedings
of that day. One is known as the Rough Journal,
and the other as the Transcript. From the latter,
as indicated by a note in the handwriting of Charles
Thomson, the Journal was printed. But in neither
is to be found a copy of the Declaration with the
signatures of the members appended, nor any copy
of the signatures. In the Rough Journal, we find
a blank space over which has been placed a printed
broadside of the Declaration, attached to the page by
red wafers. Following this, on the next page, we
read: "Ordered that the Declaration be authenti-
cated and printed. That the committee appointed to
prepare the Declaration superintend and correct the
press." This entry occurs in no other manuscript
nor in any printed Journal, and its omission is to be
explained only upon the supposition that in copying
the proceedings of the day for the printer these sentences were overlooked by the usually careful Secretary, Thomson. For, had there been any desire

to withhold them from publication, they would have appeared upon the pages of the Secret Journal, upon which they are not to be found. In the other manuscript, the Transcript, the Declaration is copied out in full in its proper place in Thomson's handwriting. From this it would appear that a copy of the manuscript of the Declaration was sent to Dunlap, the printer, immediately after the adoption of the resolution providing for its authentication and printing, and that performing his work with all possible alacrity, he had copies struck off not later than the day following that on which it was received, namely on the 5th. The authentication of this broadside, as required by vote of the Congress, was accomplished by affixing the signatures of Hancock, President, and Charles Thomson, Secretary, the words " by Order and in Behalf of the Congress," being added.

With this evidence both from print and manuscript before us, we are now in position to enter upon an examination of the question of the date of the signing. And if we are to arrive at anything approaching accuracy, all statements not strictly contemporary with the actual event must be disregarded. Nothing but additional confusion has resulted from placing reliance upon the recollections of the participants, as embodied in letters written more than forty years after the occurrences to which they refer. The memories of the Fathers are not

to be trusted for details, after the lapse of so long
a period, any more than those of ordinary mortals.
In attempting to marshal the evidence of real weight
then, we are at once struck by the fact that there are
extremely few statements of value on which reliance
can be placed.   And the further point is revealed,
that diligent search has not discovered any account
of the signing which we know took place on August
2, except the formal record in the Journal.

We have seen that the authority of prime importance, the original manuscript Journal, contains
no reference to any act of signing on July 4.   The
only entries respecting such an act are those bearing date of July 19 and August 2, as given above.
Next in importance may be considered Jefferson's
entry in his autobiography (written certainly within
a very short time after the events which he makes
note of, and perhaps even as he states " whilst these
things were going on ") wherein he records that
after the Declaration had been agreed to it was
" signed by every member present except Mr. Dickinson." [1]   This is the only direct statement to be
found that the signing took place on this day, and
as will be shown, it is manifestly incorrect.   Suffice
it to state here that Robert Morris, in addition to
Dickinson, could not have signed on that day, as
he also absented himself in order that the vote of
Pennsylvania might be cast for independence.

[1] Jefferson's *Works,* I, 28.

As against Jefferson's assertion we have three contemporary references of signal importance. Samuel Chase of Maryland signed on August 2. On July 5, when still absent from Philadelphia for the purpose of keeping Maryland in line, he wrote from Annapolis to John Adams, asking, " How shall I transmit to posterity that I gave my assent? " To this John Adams sent the well known reply on July 9, " As soon as an American Seal is prepared, I conjecture the Declaration will be subscribed by all the members, which will give you the opportunity you wish for, of transmitting your name among the votaries of independence."[1] Again, Elbridge Gerry, who had left Philadelphia on account of ill-health, twelve days after the Declaration was adopted, wrote to John and Samuel Adams from Kingsbridge, New York, on July 21, as follows: " Pray subscribe for me ye Declaration of Independency if ye same is to be signed as proposed. I think we ought to have ye privilege, when necessarily absent, of voting and signing by proxy."[2] These statements are to be interpreted in only one way, namely, that there could have been no signing on July 4, even on paper, as Jefferson contended many years later when driven into a corner.[3] No scrap or trace

[1] J. Adams, *Works,* IX, 421, and note.
[2] MS. Letter in Lenox Library, N. Y., Samuel Adams Papers.
[3] *Works,* I, 38.

of such a document has ever been discovered, nor
any reference to it except this one of Jefferson's.
As all the other documents of importance to which
signatures are attached are in existence, having been
carefully preserved by Secretary Thomson, he would
certainly not have allowed an original of such value
to have been destroyed. Taken in connection with
Chase's query and John Adams's reply, the words
of Gerry " to be signed as proposed," and " signing
by proxy " practically preclude the possibility of a
signing on July 4.

Turning now to a consideration of individual delegates who were present and might have signed on
July 4, we are confronted by the fact that had a
signing then taken place, the list would have been
strikingly different from that with which we are
familiar. New Hampshire's interests were then
looked after by Josiah Bartlett and William Whipple. Those of Massachusetts by John Hancock, the
two Adamses, Robert Treat Paine and Elbridge
Gerry. Stephen Hopkins and William Ellery represented Rhode Island, while Roger Sherman and
Samuel Huntington served Connecticut. The delegates from New York in Congress on that day were
William Floyd, Francis Lewis, George Clinton,
Henry Wisner, John Alsop, Robert R. Livingston,
Philip Livingston, and possibly, Lewis Morris.
Those from New Jersey were Richard Stockton,

John Witherspoon, Francis Hopkinson, Abraham Clark, and probably John Hart. Disturbed Pennsylvania had to put her reliance on James Wilson, Benjamin Franklin, John Morton, Thomas Willing and Charles Humphreys; and little Delaware upon Caesar Rodney, George Read, and Thomas McKean. Maryland had in Congress William Paca, Thomas Stone, and John Rogers; Virginia, Thomas Jefferson, Benjamin Harrison, Carter Braxton, and probably also Thomas Nelson, Jr., and Francis Lightfoot Lee; North Carolina, Joseph Hewes and John Penn; South Carolina, Edward Rutledge, Thomas Heyward, Jr., Thomas Lynch, Jr., and Arthur Middleton; and finally, Georgia's delegation was made up of Button Gwinnett, Lyman Hall, and George Walton. It has been possible to determine definitely that of these forty-nine men all but forty-five were in Philadelphia on July 4. As to the remaining four, though no evidence has been discovered to show that they were absent, no positive statement has been found indicating their presence. These were the men in Congress on July 4, who voted for the Declaration, and whose names would have been affixed to the paper if it had been signed on that day. Comparing them with the list of those who signed on or after August 2, marked discrepancies appear.

In the first place, as has already been stated, New York's entire delegation, for lack of instructions, even abstained from voting upon the question of independence, and assuredly would not have signed a document for which they had not voted; and George Clinton, John Alsop, R. R. Livingston, and Henry Wisner, who were in Philadelphia on July 4, but not on August 2, never affixed their signatures, though Livingston might have done so, as he attended the Congress later on for several terms. Secondly, on July 20, Pennsylvania's entire membership was rearranged, and only four of those who had represented her previous to that time, Franklin, Morris, Morton, and Wilson, were re-elected. Similar changes occurred in many of the other delegations. Passing over for the moment the names of those who were not in the Congress on August 2, when the general signing took place, we are enabled to determine that some of those whose signatures are affixed to the Declaration, could not have signed on July 4, by showing that either they were then not members of the Congress, or, if members, were absent from their posts. Thus William Williams, whose name appears among Connecticut's signers, did not reach Philadelphia until towards the end of July, having been directed to repair to that city on the eleventh, by the Council of Safety of his state.[1] Of Pennsylvania's signers, Rush, Clymer, Smith, Taylor, and Ross were

[1] *Mass. Hist. Soc. Proc.*, 2d Series, III, 375; *Force*, 5th, I, 244.

not members until July 20.[1]   Chase and Charles
Carroll, of Carrollton, were in attendance upon the
Maryland Convention at Annapolis, and were being
re-elected delegates on the very day when some suppose them to have been in Philadelphia, signing the
Declaration.[2]   Similarly George Wythe, on that day,
was chairman of the committee of the whole of the
Virginia Convention,[3] and with him was Richard
Henry Lee, who because of sickness in his family
had left Philadelphia on June 13.[4]   Again, on July 8
Hewes of North Carolina asks solicitously about the
welfare of Hooper, whom he had expected in Philadelphia long before.[5]

Attempting now to determine the names of some
of those who were present on the day officially appointed for signing the engrossed document (August
2), we reach the conclusion that a far greater number than has generally been supposed were not in
Philadelphia on that day either.   Attention has been
repeatedly drawn to the absence of Matthew Thornton and Thomas McKean.   Thornton was not elected
a member until September 2, and did not take his
seat in Congress until the fourth of the following

[1] *Journal of Congress.*
[2] *Journal of Congress,* July 18.
[3] *Force,* 4th, VI, 1608.
[4] *Ibid.,* 834.
[5] *Ibid.,* 5th, I, 117.

10

November.[1] He is differentiated from all the other
signers, in that he is the only one who took no part
in the discussion and vote on independence, and
did not arrive in Philadelphia until more than three
months after the general signing had taken place.
His signing is to be explained only by an unusually
liberal interpretation of the resolution of July 19,
which provided that after engrossment the document
should be signed by every member of the Congress.
But this resolution could not have intended that all
members subsequently elected should sign, or else a
series of extra sheets would have had to be provided
for the purpose. Colonel McKean was for a long
period absent from the Congress with his regiment,
and he is himself authority for the statement that
he signed some time in 1781.[2] And the first published list of signers, in 1777, omits his name.

But little notice has, however, been taken of no
less significant absences than these. Oliver Wolcott,
broken in health, did not remain in Philadelphia for
the final decision on independence. He knew how
his colleagues would cast the vote of their colony,
and that his continued attendance was not therefore
requisite, so he left about the end of June, and could
not have been back in Philadelphia again before the

[1] *Journal of Congress.*
[2] Buchanan's *McKean Family.*

end of September.[1] In the meantime William Williams, his substitute, had signed, and there was in reality no occasion for Wolcott to append his signature. But having taken part in the early agitation and debates he was allowed to sign under the general rule.

Elbridge Gerry, too, so important a factor in the early days of the discussion about asserting independence, who had left Philadelphia for rest and recuperation on July 16,[2] did not return until September 3,[3] a month after he is supposed to have signed. On August 24, he was at Hartford, Connecticut, and in a letter to General Gates writes that he is on his way to Philadelphia, "from which I have been absent for about a month for health."[4] The two famous Virginians, George Wythe and Richard Henry Lee, we have seen, were in Virginia on July 4. They remained there for a considerable period after that date, and were also absent from Philadelphia on August 2. On July 20, Jefferson mentions in a letter that he intends to set out on his return home not later than August 11, to visit his wife who is extremely ill, and adds that he hopes to see Lee and

[1] He was in New York on July 1 and at his home at Litchfield on July 15. *Mass. Hist. Soc. Proc.*, 2d Series, III, 374, and *Force*, 5th, I, 970.

[2] *Force*, 5th, I, 348.

[3] John Adams, *Letters to His Wife*, I, 161.

[4] *Force*, 5th, I, 1146.

Wythe in Philadelphia before he departs. On the fifth of August he deplores the fact that Lee is unable to attend until the twentieth, as it prevents his visiting Mrs. Jefferson.[1] Examining the Journal, we find that Lee's name first reappears there on August 27, and Wythe's not until nearly a month later. Lee after the earlier date and Wythe after September 23 are repeatedly selected to serve on important committees. Had they been present before, it is entirely probable that they would have been chosen for similar service, as their counsel was much sought in those days, when attendance on the Congress was slim. Lee, therefore, must have signed some time after the end of August, and Wythe probably a month later, though their signatures lead Virginia's column on the document. It is altogether likely, too, that Pennsylvania's large delegation did not all affix their signatures on the same day, as it was unusual for so many delegates from one state to be in attendance at one time. As they came and went at intervals, they probably signed whenever, after the second of August, they happened to be in attendance on the Congress.

The engrossed document is itself largely responsible for the erroneous views which have been held respecting the date of the signing. Being headed by the legend, " In Congress, July 4, 1776," and ending

[1] *Works,* II, 72, 74.

with the fifty-six signatures, the natural inference to be made, until better information was obtainable, was that this official document was signed on that day. It is further misinforming, not only as regards the date of signing, but in its title, " The unanimous Declaration of the thirteen united States," under the date July 4. For on that day, as has been shown, New York's delegates had no authority to vote, so that unanimity was procured by their silence, but twelve colonies, therefore, taking part in the final ballot. And again, seven of the names that are affixed are those of men who were not members of the Congress on July 4—Thornton, Williams, Rush, Clymer, Smith, Taylor and Ross; while exactly the same number were in the Congress on that date but never signed at any time—Clinton, Alsop, R. R. Livingston, Wisner, Willing, Humphreys and Rogers.

With all these data before us the inference is allowable that to but few men did the actual act of signing assume the large importance that it has since attained. The unanimous adoption of the Declaration was the important event, the signing a mere final touch, an after-thought. But two men, Chase and Gerry have recorded any anxiety respecting permission to sign. The others signed in accordance with the resolution passed on July 19, as a matter of course, and all except McKean, had signed when the copies of the Declaration, with the signatures of the members, were printed and distributed in accordance with the resolution of January 18, 1777.

Finally, a word may be added respecting the location of the signatures on the engrossed document. They are arranged in six columns in geographical order. Beginning at the left hand, the generous space of an entire column is given to Georgia—a treatment quite out of keeping with the extent of her efforts to support and advance independence at this time. In the next are those of North and South Carolina, followed by those of Maryland and Virginia, Pennsylvania and Delaware, New York and New Jersey. The representatives of these states having all signed, but one column more was left for all of New England, and the thirteen signatures from that region are crowded into the remaining space. When Thornton signed, there was no place for him to write his name with the New Hampshire delegation, so he was compelled to put it at the very end of the document, below the representatives of Connecticut. Nor was there room to allow for the grouping, with a space between each state, as is the case in all the other columns, except where great Pennsylvania's overwhelming numbers invade little Delaware's small allotment of territory.

If, as has been shown, there could have been no signing on July 4, this does not militate against the fact that the men who signed, and their successors in the Congress, had a full appreciation of the importance of the day. Beginning with 1777, each succeeding anniversary, during the whole period of the existence of the Continental Congress, was observed in appropriate manner with a banquet, toasts, fireworks and bonfires, and, much as we do in our time, committees were always appointed to see to it that no fitting detail was omitted that might render the occasion one of proper festivity and rejoicing.

CHAPTER VII

THE DECLARATION AND ITS CRITICS

When Thomas Jefferson penned the Declaration of Independence he could have had little notion of the fame that would be his in consequence. Nor could he have had more than a slight conception, far-seeing statesman though he was, of the ultimate influence that it was to have, not only upon the political ideas of America, but of the world as well. To say that, at home and abroad it is the most famous and familiar of our state documents, is but to record a platitude. But to seek the explanation of this fact is quite a different matter. Nor is it too much to state that, in spite of the familiar terms in which we speak of it, of the many occasions on which it has been read in public and in private, of the criticism to which it has been subjected on the one hand and the honeyed words of praise that have been heaped upon it on the other, it is within the mark, I repeat, to say that it is the least comprehended of all the great documents produced as a result of our political development.

The reason for this is not far to seek. To the people of the generation for whom it was written, it required no interpreters to make its meaning clear. It dealt with affairs that were so much of every day concern as to be entirely intelligible to all, to be thoroughly understanded of the people. But as time went by, the men to whom the Declaration made this direct, forcible, appeal passed away, leaving no precise interpretation of the commonplaces which they comprehended so clearly as to lead them to believe that all who came after must understand with like readiness. Subsequent generations assuming to understand what they did not, have thoughtlessly taken it at but a part of its full value, and even then have derived a return far in excess of the outlay of time required for its perusal. My task will be, therefore, to endeavor to put before the reader of these pages something of the aspect that the Declaration had in 1776, and the meaning it conveyed to the men of the time; in the full belief, that such an analysis will add largely to our understanding of the origin of its enormous influence, and greatly enhance rather than diminish our appreciation of it.

In the words of Professor Tyler, the endeavor to reach a right estimate of the Declaration has been hindered by the two opposite states of mind with which its consideration is approached: " on the one hand, a condition of hereditary, uncritical awe and worship of the American Revolution and of this state paper as its absolutely perfect and glorious expression; on the other hand, a later condition of cultivated distrust of the Declaration, as a piece of writing lifted up into inordinate renown by the passionate and heroic circumstances of its origin, and ever since extolled beyond reason by the blind energy of patriotic enthusiasm."[1]

Of the criticism to which it has been subjected there has been no lack, almost from the very day of its publication. " It has been attacked again and again, either in anger or contempt, by friends as well as by enemies of the American Revolution, by liberals in politics as well as by conservatives. It has been censured for its substance, it has been censured for its form; for its misstatements of fact, for its fallacies in reasoning; for its audacious novelties and paradoxes, for its total lack of all novelty, for its repetition of old and threadbare statements, even for its downright plagiarisms; finally for its grandiose and vaporing style."[2]

All the strictures passed upon the Declaration, however, meriting attention may be grouped under the heads of want of originality; of being but a mass of " glittering generalities " founded upon an impossible political philosophy, not actually believed in by the men who gave currency to it, and now a

---

[1] Tyler's *Literary Hist. of American Revolution,* I, 498.
[2] *Ibid.,* 499.

"creed outworn"; and, finally, of attacking the King with unwarranted severity, of holding him alone responsible for the commission of acts of which he was but the instrument, denouncing him without warrant as a "prince, whose character is thus marked by every act which may define a tyrant" desiring to establish an absolute tyranny over the colonists.

The all-embracing reply to be made at this point is that the Declaration has not only survived the criticism of its enemies and the adulation of its friends, but still lives a vigorous life capable of influencing unknown future generations. No document has ever been put to such severe, intimate, popular use and service. And in that use and service, had it been incapable of withstanding the test, had it contained inherent defects of serious consequence, distortions of facts as well as fallacies of reasoning, inadequency in general and in detail, it would long since have been relegated to the curiosity cabinet of the antiquarians, together with many another state paper, the product of the same time.

By the accident of circumstance it became at one and the same time the herald proclaiming the birth of our nation, and the justification for that birth as well. Combining in itself two such mighty functions, it could never have survived the severe test of time had it not been provided with human elements of a profound character. Possessing these in large degree,—far larger than we now appreciate,—throbbing with life in each of its nervous sentences, it is by this inherent vitality that it has made its appeal to the masses and the classes of men, who, not fully understanding it, yet instinctively have a respect and regard for it transcending all else in American political history. The manner of teaching our history has had some effect in crystallizing this sentiment, but no amount of teaching could have produced this had the doctrine not been worthy of its teachers. In brief, it has been put to almost every-day use, and as yet gives no evidence of suffering attrition from the contact, even though temporarily injured in one of its most vital parts as the result of the political developments of recent years.

Considering in detail the criticisms mentioned above, we find that as respects its claim to originality it was first wounded in the house of its friends. John Adams was among the earliest to find fault with it on this ground, though he could never have composed a document so terse and brief. In the evening of his days, he still smarted from a knowledge of the greater popularity of Jefferson as compared with his own. He could never get over that this idol of the people should receive

so much more of the credit for his share in the
events of the revolution than himself. Accordingly, when the Declaration had withstood nearly
a half century of assault, and reflected something
of the lustre of renown gained by its distinguished
author during his later political career, Adams
thought to accomplish the impossible by trying to
minimize its importance from the point of view of
originality. He thought to condemn it by charging
that it contained "not an idea . . . but what had
been hackneyed in Congress for two years before.
The substance of it is contained in the declaration
of rights and the violation of those rights, in the
Journals of Congress, in 1774. Indeed the essence
of it is contained in a pamphlet . . . composed by
James Otis." [1] He was entirely unaware, that in
writing these words he had missed the point completely, and was unwittingly according the Declaration the highest praise that has ever been bestowed
upon it. His criticism, which betrays a failing
strength, for in his earlier and more vigorous years
he could not have made so commonplace an observation, is one for which we should nevertheless be
grateful, since it gave Jefferson the opportunity of
penning that dignified, comprehensive, and telling
reply in which, admitting that all that Adams said

[1] *The Rights of the British Colonies Asserted and Proved*,
1764. For Adams' letter see *Works*, II, 514 note.

might be true, of which he was no judge, he adds:
" Richard Henry Lee charged it as copied from
Locke's treatise on government. Otis' pamphlet I
never saw, and whether I had gathered my ideas
from reading or reflection I do not know. I know
only that I turned to neither book nor pamphlet
while writing it. I did not consider it as any part
of my charge to invent new ideas altogether, and
to offer no sentiment which had ever been expressed
before. Had Mr. Adams been so restrained, Congress would have lost the benefit of his bold and im-
pressive advocations of the rights of Revolution.
For no man's confident and fervent addresses, more
than Mr. Adams's, encouraged and supported us
through the difficulties surrounding us, which, like
the ceaseless action of gravity, weighed on us by
night and by day. Yet, on the same ground, we
may ask what of these elevated thoughts were new,
or can be affirmed never before to have entered the
conceptions of man.

" Whether, also, the sentiments of Independence
and the reasons for declaring it, which make so
great a portion of the instrument, had been hackneyed in Congress for two years before the fourth of
July, '76, . . . let history say. This, however, I
will say for Mr. Adams, that he supported the Declaration with zeal and ability, fighting fearlessly for
every word of it. As to myself, I thought it a

duty to be, on that occasion, a passive auditor of the opinions of others, more impartial judges than I could be, of its merits or demerits. During the debate I was sitting by Doctor Franklin, and he observed that I was writhing a little under the acrimonious criticisms on some of its parts ; and it was on that occasion, that by way of comfort, he told me the story of John Thompson the hatter and his new sign."[1]

No words by way of explanation or in addition can diminish or increase the force of this calm presentation of Jefferson's conception of the task before him, nor any serve as completer answer to the charge made. Originality of substance was the last quality the Declaration should have had if it was adequately to subserve its purpose.

Of the utter failure to comprehend the true significance and meaning of the Declaration, on the part of the later generations, no better example exists than that furnished by the renowned advocate Rufus Choate, who in 1856 first spoke of " the glittering and sounding generalities of natural right which make up the Declaration of Independence."[2] This high-sounding phrase, as rhetorical as any part of the instrument which it seeks to criticise, has been quoted with such constant repetition and approval

[1] Jefferson's *Works*, X, 267–268.
[2] *Letter to the Whigs of Maine*, 1856.

as to have contributed an idiom to our language. For that service alone it should be welcomed. If, however, this characterization is to be regarded as giving in any degree an adequate summary of the Declaration, as is assumed by the author of the most substantial of the recent histories of American literature,[1] its falsity will become apparent from a reading of the analysis supplied in the succeeding chapters. In the sense, however, that by the glitter of its golden phrases the Declaration to some extent blinded the men of the time, and prevented them from perceiving the full magnitude of the contest in which they were about to engage, Mr. Choate's words are measurably true. But such was not the idea he wished to convey, and such is not the understanding of those who have given his thought a currency that no counterfeit should have procured. He viewed it from its rhetorical side alone, overlooking the deep underlying basis of fact that it contained. In so doing he failed to discern that the leaders in the Congress at that time, had other occupations than signing their names to documents that were mere pieces of rhetoric. That the Declaration contains rhetorical passages none can deny, but that it is all idle vaporing no one familiar with the history of the antecedent controversy, and the pointed references of each of its clauses, can admit. Moreover, the constant use and

[1] Wendell's *Literary History of America,* 106.

service to which the Declaration has been put, have
caused its fundamental concepts to assume something of the nature of generalities to the masses of
men. This is the natural consequence from the
universal acceptance of maxims which at one time
had to prove their quality before obtaining standing.
By the vast advances made in recent years in scientific method, many old and cherished theories of past
ages have been uprooted. The political ideas of the
Fathers seem no more likely to survive than any
other part of the philosophy of their time. This is
natural, since in a dynamic society the discovery of
new phenomena must give rise to new interpretations
of them. But so far little conscious, discernible impress has been made by the latter-day doctrines of
political science upon our political life. The whole
body of the science is as yet too new to have done
so, and until it has proved its mettle through trial,
the masses of men will continue, certainly in this
country, to adhere with tenacity to the old doctrines that have served as inspiration to so many
generations. And just as the political philosophy of
the eighteenth century now seems outworn, and has
been supplanted by the evolutionary philosophy, so
the latter will in all likelihood prove to be no more
the final word upon the subject than its predecessor.

The answer to the charge of indicting merely the
King when Parliament was as much to blame for the

11

maladministration of American affairs as himself,
has to some extent been given in the earlier pages.
To have now held Parliament, or Parliament and
King jointly, and not the King alone, responsible for
the act which they were driven to commit, would
have been to stultify the whole course of procedure
of the colonies in the controversy.   From its incep-
tion it was based on opposition to the ministry and
Parliament, and on the assumption that the King and
his acts were to be differentiated from the former.[1]
It began with the denial of the right of Parliament
to have control over the colonies, not only in matters
of taxation but in general affairs as well, except so
far as was necessary to promote the welfare of the
British empire.   Fundamentally it had its origin in
the concept that the rights to life, liberty, and property, and " the rights, liberties and immunities of
free and natural born subjects,"[2] were the colonists'
by inheritance, and had been guaranteed to them
" by the plighted faith of government and the most
solemn compacts with British sovereigns "—not, it
is to be noted, with the British Parliament.[3]   They

---

[1] See in this connection the early attempts in Pennsylvania
to overthrow the proprietary government with the object of
having the colony converted into a royal province under the
crown.   Sheperd, *Hist. of Prop. Govt. in Penna. passim,*
Lincoln, *op. cit.,* Chapter VI.

[2] *Declaration of Rights,* 1774.

[3] *Address to People of Great Britain,* Oct. 21, 1774.

held further, that the " foundation of English liberty, and of all free government, is a right in the people to participate in their legislative council: and as the English colonists are not represented, and from their local and other circumstances, cannot properly be represented in the British Parliament, they are entitled to a free and exclusive power of legislation in the several provincial legislatures, where their right of representation can alone be preserved, in all cases of taxation and internal polity, subject only to the negative of their sovereign, in such manner as has been heretofore used and accustomed." But from the necessity of the case, they would submit to the regulation of their external commerce " for the purpose of securing the commercial advantages of the whole empire, to the mother country . . . excluding every idea of taxation internal or external, for raising a revenue on the subjects in America, without their consent."[1]

This then was their theory: the social contract idea of the origin of government, on which their relations with the British empire were based; the right to representation, and through their representatives the control of their property, subject only to a limited, vague, ill-defined, parliamentary supervision. A considerable number of the more logical, among them notably Jefferson, prior to the meeting

[1] *Declaration of Rights,* 1774, Article 4.

of the Congress of 1774, had gone further, and dis-
claiming the authority of Parliament to bind the
colonies in any respect whatever, spoke of the " acts
of power, assumed by a body of men, foreign to our
constitutions and unacknowledged by our laws."[1]
But since they admitted that full allegiance was
owing to the crown, by reason of solemn compact,
this was not seriously called in question in any document, except in one paragraph of the address to the
colonies of October, 1774,[2]—and this may be assumed to be a slip. Going further, they stated ex-
plicitly in their first petition that they desired no
diminution of the royal prerogative. Though how
they could reconcile this with some of the passages
in the address to the colonies of 1774, is not quite
clear. However, entire consistency was never a
characteristic of any revolution.

On the other hand the " legislature," " parliament," " the ministry," and " administration," are
repeatedly denounced and held responsible for the
ills from which they are suffering.[3] As has been
shown, the first occasion on which official expression
was given to the grounds on which the United Col-

[1] *Summary View,* Ford's *Jefferson,* I, 439.

[2] *Journal,* October 21, 1774. The sentence begins, " By order of the King."

[3] *Address to People of Great Britain,* and *Address to Colonies,* 1774. *Declaration of Causes of Taking up Arms,* July
6, 1775, etc.

onies would base their contentions, and the lengths
to which Parliament was to be allowed to go in exercising control, was in the Declaration of Rights
of 1774. The very fact of determining then to issue
addresses to the King, and to the people of Great
Britain and America, with studied care ignoring Parliament from now on, except to denounce it, was in
itself a renunciation of parliamentary supremacy
more bold than any of the Congress' other measures.
Nine months later, after again professing a willingness to submit to the acts of trade and navigation
passed before 1763, the position of Congress was re-
stated in the very words used before.[1] In the official
answer to Lord North's motion, in the main the
handiwork of Jefferson,[2] made a few weeks later,
such paragraphs as this are found: " As the colonies
possess a right of appropriating their gifts, so are
they entitled at all times to inquire into their application. . . . To propose, therefore, as this resolution
does, that the moneys given by the colonies shall be
subject to the disposal of parliament alone, is to propose that they shall relinquish this right of inquiry,
and put it in the power of others to render their
gifts ruinous, in proportion as they are liberal."
Again: "We conceive that the British parliament has

[1] July 8, 1775, *Address to the Inhabitants of Great Britain.*
[2] *Works*, I, 18, 476. See p. 39, *supra. Journal of Congress,*
July 31, 1775.

no right to intermeddle with our provisions for the support of civil government, or administration of justice. . . . While parliament pursues their plan of civil government within their own jurisdiction, we also hope to pursue ours without molestation." And a little further on in the same document we find an enumeration of the acts which can never be submitted to since they evince a desire for " the exercise of indiscriminate legislation over us."

Side by side with these disclaimers of parliamentary supremacy went protests of the most absolute loyalty to the King.[1] And as if to render them the more forcible, they are accompanied by unequivocal denials that their conduct is actuated by a desire to separate from the British union and establish an independent government.[2] The unprepared condition of the country for war, is the best proof of the truth of these assertions, as well as the strongest answer to those who maintain that the whole agitation was but a veil to cloak a movement having as its ultimate object the establishment of independence. The country was not more prepared for independence than it was for war, at this time, a year before the final act was consummated, and had any idea of separation from the mother country been definitely announced, it would have wrecked the whole revolu-

[1] Petitions of 1774 and 1775.
[2] *Journal*, July 6, 1775.

tionary organization. Scarcely half a dozen of the members of the Congress favored it, and they were the radicals among radicals, and their weakness was demonstrated by the overwhelming manner in which their opposition to sending a second petition was brushed aside.

The definite renunciation of all idea of parliamentary control of any kind came in December, 1775, in answer to the King's proclamation of August 23[1] —the sole reply ever accorded to their last petition. In this we find also the most definite statement of the colonial view of the relations between the crown and the colonies, as yet put forward. Moreover, the wager of battle thrown down by the King is taken up, and now for the first time the rights of the crown are seriously called into question. In the King's proclamation the colonists were accused of " forgetting the allegiance which they owe to the power that has protected and maintained them." To this the reply is made: " What allegiance is it that we forgot? Allegiance to parliament? We never owed—we never owned it. . . . We condemn, and with arms in our hands, a resource which freemen will never part with, we oppose the claim and exercise of unconstitutional powers, to which neither the crown nor parliament were ever entitled. . . . We know of no laws binding on us, but such as have been trans-

[1] See p. 47.

mitted to us by our ancestors, and such as have been consented to by ourselves."

The time had arrived, now, to take a further step in the enunciation of the theory on which the opposition to the British contentions was based. This was done in the document cited above in the following specific and thoroughly adequate terms from the point of view of English constitutional history: " We view him [the king] as the constitution represents him. That tells us he can do no wrong. The cruel and illegal attacks, which we oppose, have no foundation in the royal authority. We will not on our part lose the distinction between the King and his ministers; happy would it have been for some former princes, had it always been preserved on the part of the crown."[1] And in thus emphasizing the view that Parliament and the ministry were distinct from the crown, they were but giving voice to the doctrine of the separation of powers first announced by Locke, and more recently made familiar in the well-known work of Montesquieu, which every political thinker of this time had at his elbow.

Thus, having constantly drawn the distinction between the King on the one hand, and the ministry and Parliament on the other, and having already repudiated the ministry and Parliament in the terms

[1] This remarkably strong paper was drawn up by R. H. Lee, Wilson, and W. Livingston.

recorded in the last few pages, there was nothing left for the colonies but to renounce, at the last stage, their allegiance to the crown. This was done for the first time in the resolutions of May 15, 1776,[1] and finally, and for all time, in the Declaration of Independence. By way of concluding the discussion of this point the words of Daniel Webster, who has so clearly interpreted the colonial position, may well be reproduced here: " The inhabitants of all the colonies, while colonies, admitted themselves bound by their allegiance to the King; but they disclaimed altogether, the authority of Parliament; holding themselves, in this respect to resemble the condition of Scotland and Ireland, before the respective unions of those kingdoms with England, when they acknowledged allegiance to the same King, but each had its separate legislature. The tie therefore, which our revolution was to break, did not subsist between us and the British government, in the aggregate; but directly between us and the King himself. The colonists had never admitted themselves subject to Parliament. That was precisely the point of the original controversy. They had uniformly denied that Parliament had authority to make laws for them. There was, therefore, no subjection to Parliament to be thrown off. But allegiance to the King did exist, and had been uni-

[1] See p. 91.

formly acknowledged; and down to 1775, the most solemn assurances had been given that it was not intended to break that allegiance, or to throw it off. Therefore, as the direct object, and only effect of the Declaration, according to the principles on which the controversy had been maintained, was to sever the tie of allegiance which bound us to the King, it was properly and necessarily founded on acts of the crown itself, as its justifying causes. . . . Consistency with the principles upon which resistance began, and with all the previous state papers issued by Congress required that the Declaration should be bottomed on the misgovernment of the King; and therefore it was properly framed with that aim and to that end. The King was known indeed, to have acted, as in other cases, by his ministers, and with his Parliament; but as our ancestors had never admitted themselves subject either to ministers or Parliament, there were no reasons to be given for now refusing obedience to their authority. This clear and obvious necessity of founding the Declaration on the misconduct of the King himself, gives to that instrument its personal application, and its character of direct and pointed accusation." [1]

To so much as concerns the charges in the Declaration respecting the establishment of an ab-

[1] *Speech in Fancuil Hall,* Boston, Aug. 2, 1826.

solute tyranny, and of a conduct, " marked by every act which may define a tyrant," but few words, in passing, are necessary. If the charges against the king had any basis in fact, they assuredly displayed a desire to establish a tyranny, as that term is understood in English constitutional history, and as it is defined by Locke. And the personal dominance which George III established over his Parliament and ministers, dating from 1768, by the most corrupt methods debauching the whole of the ruling classes for his own purposes,[1] was marked, if not " by every act which may define a tyrant," at least by sufficient to warrant recourse to that rhetorical characterization, when the exigencies of the occasion made requisite.

[1] See Lecky, *Hist. of England in 18th Century,* and Green, *Short Hist. of English People.* Also Donne's *Correspondence of George III with Lord North.*

CHAPTER VIII

The Purpose of the Declaration

Consideration having been given to the erroneous conceptions respecting the Declaration, that have arisen as the result of approaching it with inadequate preparation for its proper understanding, it is necessary at this point to give attention to the purpose it was intended to subserve, and to regard it from the point of view of the success with which this was attained. For the accomplishment of this object it is requisite that so far as possible it be interpreted, not in terms of twentieth century philosophy or politics, but from the standpoint of the men who had a share in the events from which the Declaration arose, and of which it was, to an extent, the outward expression. No part of the writing of history is more difficult than that which aims to put ourselves in the place of the men participating in great historic movements, and to attempt to view the results of their achievements from their own attitude of mind, to penetrate the well-springs of their motives. Yet, unless this be undertaken, no substantially correct results can be achieved. Accordingly it is for us to consider now the motives actuating Jefferson's selection to prepare the Declaration, and the nature of the task put before him.

The stupendous magnitude of the work was appreciated by none so well as by him, and might readily have caused even a greater man to hesitate long before engaging in it. Yet the choice of the Congress, and of the committee fell upon him, with singular unanimity, as the one best fitted by his attainments to produce a document of the character desired. This was no mere chance, for, though his voice was silent, his pen had given full expression to his thoughts. He was no orator, but, " a silent member in Congress," yet " prompt, frank, explicit, and decisive upon committees and in conversation."[1]

Among all the countless disquisitions upon the rights of the colonies, and the wrongs to which the colonists believed they had been subjected, produced during the previous fifteen years of controversy, one, written in 1774, and given the title *A Summary View of the Rights of British America,*[2] stood out in especial prominence, marking its author as a greater among great men. Jefferson designed it to serve the double purpose of furnishing instructions to the Virginia delegates to the first

[1] J. Adams' *Works,* II, 514, note.
[2] Ford's *Jefferson,* I, 421 *et seq.*

Continental Congress, and to give that body a common ground on which to establish its statement of grievances and demands for redress. That in some of its contentions it was too advanced to be suitable to the exigencies of the time and failed of its object, is not of importance in this connection. But it is to the point, that it displayed a scholarly knowledge of the history of the various colonies, a depth of insight into the essentials of the controversy, framed withal with a felicity and lucidity of expression, such as was possessed by none of his contemporaries. In the brief twenty-three pages of this essay he touched upon every phase of the colonial contentions, and thereby established his reputation as a forceful, sagacious, philosophical thinker.[1]

To prepare a Declaration of Independence, however, was a far different task. That document, in a few lines, had to cover not only all the ground of the *Summary View*, but to recapitulate as well the rapid developments of the two full years that had elapsed since its production. As it was designed to appeal to all the colonies, it had to treat not only of the grievances common to all, but of those that bore most heavily upon any particular colony, were peculiar to that colony, and consequently of transcending importance to itself. Yet

[1] See also his proposed constitution for Virginia, *Works*, II, 7 *et seq.*

in so doing the balance of the whole had to be carefully preserved, that no single part might rise to undue prominence by the over-weight of any other. But it could not stop here. It had to be couched in such terms as would serve as justification, to the world at large no less than to the inhabitants of the colonies, for the act which it proclaimed. Dealing with things familiar to every frequenter of the taverns, to every reader of the gazettes and pamphlets, it had to make its appeal to the thoughtful as well as to the unthinking, to the philosophers as well as to the groundlings, and in such a manner that they would not be wearied by its perusal, but stirred to enthusiasm as they proceeded. It had to include the best of the previous productions, but only their essentials. Not less a party platform of national scope than a political manifesto, the warmth of its phraseology must win over the wavering and fire the more advanced with a desire to come forward to enlist and fight for their rights and liberties, since troops were at this time much more needed than wordy rhetoric. As such it took the place of the " animated address," resolved upon at the end of May, which was " to impress the minds of the people with the necessity of now stepping forward to save their country, their freedom, and property," but which never saw the

light, since the issuance of the Declaration made
this unnecessary.[1]

All these qualities it must have and more besides.
It must foster the rapidly advancing though far from
strong sentiment of union, so that those who once
gave assent to it would support each other no matter
what the future had in store for them. And it must
needs do this in such manner that no other course
should appear practicable. It was to be the expression of a minority party, but of so well-organized
a minority, that it could hope ultimately to effect the
conversion of that party, by accessions to its ranks,
into an unquestioned, dominating majority. It
could not, therefore, be non-partisan, yet it must con-
vince by argument as well as drive by force of its
inherent power. And no slight portion of its
strength was to be gained from couching it in a
phraseology made familiar during the fifteen years
of controversy, and having a basis in the whole of
English and colonial constitutional development. It
had to make charges, but none that could not be
reasonably supported; and in indicting a King and a
nation it had to word this indictment in such terms
that it would not be thrown out of court by the country and the world. The position of the revolutionists

---

[1] *Secret Journal of Congress, Domestic,* May 29, 1776. The
committee to prepare this address consisted of Jefferson,
Wythe, S. Adams and Rutledge.

had to be fortified so that it could withstand attack, and, having the choice of situation, it had to make the most of the enemy's weakness, nor yet disregard its strength.

Since it was to be, as has been well said by Professor Tyler, " an impassioned manifesto of one party, and that the weaker party in a violent race quarrel; of a party resolved, at last, upon the extremity of a revolution, and already menaced by the inconceivable disaster of being defeated in the very act of armed rebellion against the mightiest power on earth," it " is not to be censured because being avowedly a statement of its side of the quarrel, it does not also contain a moderate and judicial statement of the opposite side; or because, being necessarily partisan in method, it is likewise both partisan and vehement in tone."[1]   Jefferson's position was that of advocate, and he so regards himself, and it was his duty, therefore, to present his case in the strongest possible terms, leaving his opponent to take care of himself.

But above all, had the Declaration comprised all the qualities which have been mentioned as necessary to its fulfilling the objects for which it was designed, it would never have survived as it has, and attained to its vast influence upon our political life, had it been lacking in three essential characteristics. These

[1] *Literary Hist. of American Revolution,* I, 509.

are its underlying philosophy, its human elements, and its literary form. Of the philosophy more will be said presently. Suffice it now to call attention to the fact that it had been preached to such an extent, that through the Declaration it could make its appeal direct to the mind of even the most unthinking. The human element of the Declaration appears in almost every phrase, from the first respecting the refusal of assent to laws most wholesome and necessary for the public good, to the last of exciting domestic insurrection and endeavoring to bring on the inhabitants of the frontiers, the merciless Indian savages. Had it not been possible thus to address the emotions of the individual and make him feel that his all was at stake, and had it not been done in such forceful, stirring, convincing manner, the revolution could never have been carried to a successful conclusion.

No one is better qualified to speak of the literary form of the Declaration than Professor Tyler. The praise he accords it is of the highest, but none familiar with his scholarly attainments will regard it as undiscriminating or lavish. " Most writings," he holds, " have had the misfortune of being read too little. There is however a misfortune—perhaps a greater misfortune—which has overtaken some literary compositions, and these not necessarily the noblest and best, of being read too much. At any

rate, the writer of a piece of literature which has
been neglected, need not be refused the consolation
he may get from reflecting that he is, at least, not
the writer of a piece of literature that has become
hackneyed. Just this is the sort of calamity which
seems to have befallen the Declaration of Independence. . . .

" Had the Declaration of Independence, been, what
many a revolutionary state paper is, a clumsy, ver-
bose and vaporing production, not even the robust
literary taste and the all-forgiving patriotism of the
American people could have endured the weariness,
the nausea, of hearing its repetition, in ten thousand
different places, at least once every year for so long
a period. Nothing which has not supreme literary
merit has ever triumphantly endured such an ordeal,
or ever been subjected to it. No man can adequately
explain the persistent fascination which this state
paper has had, and which it still has, for the American people, or for its undiminishing power over
them, without taking into account its extraordinary
literary merits—its possession of the witchery of
true substance wedded to perfect form : its massive-
ness and incisiveness of thought, its art in the mar-
shalling of the topics with which it deals, its sym-
metry, its energy, the definiteness and limpidity of
its statements, its exquisite diction—at once terse,
musical, and electrical ; and as an essential part of

this literary outfit, many of those spiritual notes which can attract and enthrall our hearts, veneration for God, veneration for man, veneration for principle, respect for public opinion, moral earnestness, moral courage, optimism, a stately and noble pathos, finally, self-sacrificing devotion to a cause so great as to be herein identified with the happiness, not of one people only, or of one race only, but of human nature itself."[1]

If the Declaration be adjudged as reaching the high standards, and fulfilling the variety of purposes here set forth, with success even measurable, it will be admitted that few other public documents can be subjected to such a trial and emerge in triumph. Yet as the attempt is being made to view it from the aspect of the men to whom it was intended to appeal, so their opinion of it is of primary value. Amid the general chorus of approval with which it was acclaimed by the leaders, not less than by the rank and file of the party to whom it was directed, but one voice of strength in opposition is raised sufficiently loud to be heard. Robert Morris, in a letter to his friend Joseph Reed, gave as his reason for voting against and opposing the Declaration that "it was an improper time, and will neither promote the interests nor redound to the honor of America; for it has caused division when we wanted

[1] Tyler, I, 519–521.

union, and will be ascribed to very different principles than those which sought to give rise to such an important measure." [1] And here, it may be added, the opposition rests upon the opportuneness of the act, rather than the manner of its consummation. As against this, we may put the calm opinion of Washington, expressed in acknowledging to Hancock the receipt of the Declaration: "It is certain that it is not with us to determine in many instances what consequences will flow from our counsels; but yet it behooves us to adopt such, as, under the smiles of a gracious and all-kind Providence will be most likely to promote our happiness. I trust the late decisive part they have taken is calculated to that end, and will secure to us that freedom and those privileges, which have been and are refused to us, contrary to the voice of nature and the British constitution." When proclaimed before all the army under his command, the Declaration received " their most hearty assent: the expressions and behaviour of both officers and men, testifying their warmest approbation of it."[1] To Schuyler he spoke of it as an act " impelled by necessity, and a repetition of injuries no longer sufferable, and being without the most distant prospect of relief, they [Congress] have asserted the claims of the colonies

[1] Reed's *Reed,* I, 201, July 20, 1776.
[2] Sparks' *Washington,* III, 457.

to the rights of humanity, absolved them from all
allegiance to the British crown, and declared them
Free and Independent States." [1]   And in his orders
to the army, he spoke of it as having been impelled
" by the dictates of duty, policy, and necessity." [2]
The more enthusiastic Samuel Adams declared it
" has given vigour to the spirits of the people." [3]
His younger kinsman, John Adams, spoke of it as
" a Declaration setting forth the causes which have
impelled us to this mighty revolution, and the reasons which will justify it in the sight of God and
man," [4] and again, as likely to " cement the Union,
and avoid those heats, and perhaps convulsions,
which might have been occasioned by such a declaration six months ago." [5]   And William Whipple
tells us that " This declaration has had a glorious
effect—has made these colonies all alive : all the Colonies forming Governments, as you will see by the
papers."   And in another letter, dated a few days
later, he writes : " This Colony [6] and New Jersey are
all alive . . . men of fortune don't think themselves
too good to march in the character of private soldiers . . . —in short the Declaration of Independ-

[1] *Ibid.,* 464.
[2] *Ibid.,* 458.
[3] *Force,* 5th, I, 347.
[4] *Works,* IX, 418.
[5] *Ibid.,* 420.
[6] Pennsylvania.

ence has done wonders."[1]   Josiah Bartlett, in welcoming the adoption of the Declaration by New York, rejoiced that it now had " the sanction of the Thirteen United States," adding, that " the unparalleled conduct of our enemies have united the colonies more firmly than ever."[2]

Such was the high esteem in which both the act and the expression of it were held by the leaders of the time, and if to them it seemed adequate to the great occasion, we should accept their opinion as the final word. True, the Declaration of Independence and the ultimate acknowledgment of our national existence were separated by many trying years of weary contest, and the issue seemed more than once suspended in the balance by a mere thread. But this does not alter the fact that the Declaration of Independence was regarded as an opportune and comprehensive statement of the reasons impelling to that act at the time, that without it open assistance from France was not to be procured, and that after its proclamation no overtures looking to a conclusion of the struggle were for a moment considered, that were not based on public acknowledgment of the United States as an independent nation.

[1] *Langdon-Elwyn Papers*, Lenox Library, New York, 139–140. The letter is dated July 22, 1776.
[2] *Force*, 5th, I, 348.

CHAPTER IX

THE PHILOSOPHY OF THE DECLARATION

" Happy is the nation," writes Sir Leslie Stephen, " which has no political philosophy, for such a philosophy is generally the offspring of a recent or the symptom of an approaching revolution."[1] The philosophy of the American Revolution, though representative of the latter concept, has underlying it the story of a political development that has its roots deep down in English history of the seventeenth century. That was the age of intellectual and political revolt in England, which attained its final fruition in the following century in America. The Puritan Revolution stirred the political sense of the nation not less than its religious emotions. The intensive study which the Old Testament received in consequence, reacted in marked degree upon the political ideas of the time. As Borgeaud aptly puts it, " the first political manifestoes of modern democracy were formulated in England in the seventeenth century and they were the fruit of the religious revolutions caused by the Reformation."[2]

[1] *English Thought in the 18th Century*, 3d ed., II, 131.
[2] *Rise of Modern Democracy in Old and New England*, 105.

184

The theories of natural rights and the origin of government in contract had their rise at this time. Men were then more prone than now to seek for evidences of the Divine Hand in the institution of mundane affairs. And as ideas of government, lay and clerical, were receiving earnest study and new application, their origins were sought for in the sacred books. In these were to be found the earliest recorded instances of the genesis of government. With minds open to interpretations that fell in with preconceived views, the covenants recorded as made between God and the Jewish people, were seized upon as proof-positive of the contractual nature of the first governmental forms.[1] With circumstances arising to give their thoughts ready employment, it is not to be wondered that the contract theory was applied on the one side by Hobbes to bolster up the divine authority of kings, on the other by Locke to give warrant to the supremacy of the legislative arm of the government as the direct representative of the people.

If, therefore, we would seek out the immediate sources of the political philosophy of the American Revolution, we must look for them in the history of

---

[1] I am aware of the learned treatise by Dr. Sullivan (*Rept. Am. Hist. Assn.*, 1903, Vol. I, 67 *et seq.*) tracing the social compact idea through classical and mediæval authors. But they did not have so immediate an effect at this time as the Old Testament.

English thought in the seventeenth century, and in the great state papers which clothed it in constitutional form.[1] The principal expounders of the political philosophy of this period were Hooker, Hobbes and Locke, and their very names are indicative of the historical events to which they gave literary expression. All of them based the origin of government upon a social contract, the outgrowth of a time when life in a state of nature no more proved feasible. To Hooker and Hobbes the state of nature was a condition of anarchy, of warfare and constant strife, to end which men established forms of government. To Locke, on the contrary, it was a "golden age," and political societies were created to protect and secure persons and property, when men became corrupt and no longer respected each other's rights.

As Hobbes reflected the spirit of the Puritan Revolution,[2] so Locke "expounded the principles of the Revolution of 1688, and his writings became the

[1] See in this connection, besides the works of Hooker, Hobbes, Locke, Sydney, and the political writings of Milton, the excellent and suggestive study by A. L. Lowell in his *Essays on Government,* Merriam's *Am. Pol. Theories,* Sir Leslie Stephens' *English Thought in the 18th Century,* Sir James Fitzjames Stephens' *Horæ Sabbaticæ,* Vols. II and III, Bryce's *Studies in History and Jurisprudence,* McLaughlin in *Am. Hist. Rev.,* Vol. V, No. 3, 467 *et seq.,* and Ritchie's *Natural Rights.*

[2] The *Leviathan* appeared in 1651.

political bible of the following century, the source from which later writers drew their arguments, and the authority to which they appealed in default of arguments."[1] And just as the events of 1688 and the final establishment of the supremacy of Parliament could not have occurred without the previous period of revolution and reaction, so Locke's *Treatises on Government* (issued in 1690), it may safely be said, would never have seen the light of day had he not lived through this formative time, and had the thoughts of Hooker and Hobbes and Sir Robert Filmer not been set down to spur him on to the expression of his views. Since Locke proved the " formal expounder of Whiggism "[2] in America to a greater extent even than in England, it is to his ideas that it will prove most profitable to devote attention. " His chief influence," it has been well said, " was in popularizing a convenient formula for enforcing the responsibility of governors,"[3] and his arguments were not less familiar to every political thinker and writer in America, than was the Old Testament to the Old and New England Puritans.

Beginning in his second *Treatise* (the first being entirely devoted to a labored refutation of Filmer's *Patriarcha*) with a consideration of the state of na-

---

[1] Sir Leslie Stephen, *op. cit.,* II, 135.

[2] *Ibid.*

[3] *Ibid.*, 143.

ture, he proceeds to discuss the purposes of political
or civil society and their beginnings, the forms of
commonwealths, the powers of the several branches
of governments (placing the treatment of the legislative power in advance of that of the executive),
and then, after treating in order such subjects as
the prerogative, conquest, usurpation and tyranny,
he concludes most appropriately with an elaborate
chapter on the dissolution of governments.

In the state of nature, men are in a condition of
"perfect freedom to order their actions and dis-
pose of their possessions and persons as they think
fit, within the bounds of the law of nature."
Further, "it is a state of equality wherein all the
power and jurisdiction is reciprocal, no one having
more than another." This state, however, "though
a state of liberty, is not a state of license." "It has
a law to govern it which obliges every one, and reason, which is that law, teaches all mankind who will
but consult it, that being all equal and independent
no one ought to harm another in his life, health,
property, or possessions,"—the "unalienable rights"
of the Declaration of Independence. The law of
nature confers upon man, therefore, all the rights of
person and property. It is not to acquire property
rights that man enters into political society, but in
order to protect and secure those he already has,
to avoid the destructive state of war that may arise

at any time, and to remedy the inconveniences that have grown up in the state of nature.

Thus " men being by nature all free, equal, and independent, no one can be put out of this estate, and subjected to the political power of another, without his own consent." As soon as men agree to associate to form a political society, they enter into a social compact with each other, and consent to be guided by the will of the majority to make and execute laws for the general good. " Property," in Locke's conception, is used in a very extensive sense; it comprises all rights of any nature, especially those of a personal character, and it is the product of man's own labor.

As to the forms of government, he makes the familiar classification into monarchies, aristocracies and democracies, and then gives consideration to the various branches of government. Of these the legislative is all-important, mirroring thus the Whig view of the supremacy of Parliament as against the Stuart contention of the divine right of kings. " This legislative is not only the supreme power of the commonwealth, but sacred and unalterable in the hands where community have once placed it." But, though the legislative is supreme, " and therefore all obedience, which by the most solemn ties any one can be obliged to pay, ultimately terminates in this supreme power, and is directed by those laws

which it enacts," it is none the less subject to four
limitations. First, it can not be "absolutely arbitrary over the lives and fortunes of the people," since
"nobody can transfer to another more power than
he has in himself, and nobody has an absolute arbitrary power over himself, or over any other, to
destroy his own life, or take away the life or property of another." "Secondly, the legislative or supreme authority cannot assume to itself a power to
rule by extemporary, arbitrary decrees, but is bound
to dispense justice and decide the rights of the subject by promulgated standing laws, and known authorized judges." For "absolute arbitrary power,
or governing without settled standing laws, can
neither of them consist with the ends of society and
government, which men would not quit the state
of nature for, and tie themselves up under, were it
not to preserve their lives, liberties and fortunes."
"Thirdly, the supreme power cannot take from any
man any part of his property without his own consent," since the very aim of government is to preserve property, and if it be taken away without consent "they have no property at all." This idea of
the consent to the appropriation of property as fundamental, is elaborated with much particularity, and
in his recapitulation is re-stated thus: "They must
not raise taxes on the property of the people without
the consent of the people, given by themselves or

their deputies." " Fourthly, the legislative cannot transfer the power of making laws to any other hands, for it being but a delegated power from the people, they who have it can not pass it over to others . . . nor can they be bound by any laws but such as are enacted by those whom they have chosen and authorized to make laws for them."

Next he discusses the relations of the legislative and the executive to the people. The executive he makes dependent upon the legislative, and over them both " there remains still in the people a supreme power to remove or alter the legislative, when they find the legislative act contrary to the trust reposed in them." The prerogative of the executive, though necessarily extensive, has bounds set to it by the laws made by the legislative; since " prerogative can be nothing but the people's permitting their rulers to do several things of their own free choice where the law was silent, . . . for the public good and their acquiescing in it when so done." Having next put limits to the right of conquest which he calls " a foreign usurpation," he considers usurpation which " is a kind of domestic conquest, with this difference—that an usurper can never have right on his side, it being no usurpation but when one is got into the possession of what another has right to." Of tyranny, he says, " whosoever in authority exceeds the power given him by the law, and makes use of the forces he has under his command, to compass that upon the subject which the law allows not, ceases in that to be a magistrate; and acting without authority, may be opposed as any other man who by force invades the right of another."

The concluding chapter on the " dissolution of governments" is thus led up to. For this two causes may be assigned. The first occurs when by the arbitrary will of " a single person or prince," the legislative is altered, by setting up his own will in its place, by hindering its time and place of meeting and freedom of action, or by changing the " ways of election . . . without the consent or contrary to the common interest of the people." The alternative cause of dissolution occurs when the legislative and the prince act contrary to their trust, " when they endeavor to invade the property of the subject, and to make themselves, or any part of the community masters or arbitrary disposers of the lives, liberties or fortunes of the people." " Whenever the legislators endeavor to take away and destroy the property of the people, or to reduce them to slavery under arbitrary power, they put themselves into a state of war with the people, who are thereupon absolved from any further obedience, and are left to the common refuge which God hath provided for all men against force and violence. Whenever, therefore, the legislative shall trangress this fundamental rule of society, and either by ambition, fear, folly, or corruption, endeavor to grasp themselves, or put into the hands of any other, an absolute power over the lives, liberties and estates of the people; by this breach of trust they forfeit the power the people had put into their hands for quite contrary ends, and it devolves to the people, who have a right to resume their original liberty, and by the establishment of a new legislative (such as they shall think fit), provide for their own safety and security, which is the end for which they are in society."

Such is, in outline, the theory of government as expounded by John Locke. It displays in almost every part the doctrines made familiar by the Revolution of 1688. Moreover, as the political excitement died down in England with the settlement in 1689 of the great question that had agitated the country for half a century, and as the Whigs, the exponents of these ideas, were in almost constant power until the accession of George III, contributing so greatly to the ascendancy of the country, there naturally ensued a period of political contentment. During this, as the supremacy of Parliament had been established, the theory of the social compact and of the division of the powers of government was gradually lost sight of, so that when a forceful monarch like George III came to the throne, he was able by his dominating personality and his easy con-

13

science to make himself practical dictator, within the bounds of the British constitution.

But in America other conditions produced different results. In the nearly seventy years succeeding the Revolution of 1688, great problems of government were being worked out anew. That period saw the evolution of the legislature in all the colonies to a position of authority greater almost within its confined limits, than had been attained by Parliament at home. And whereas the conditions in England allowed of the predominance of a forceful individual over the will of the nation, the more democratic character of political institutions in America saw the ever-increasing strengthening of the will of the people through their legislatures. During all this period parliamentary authority was little exercised over the colonies, while, on the other hand, much controversy arose between the King, as one party to a compact (of which the charters were the outward expression), and the colonists through their legislatures as the other. The colonists came to ignore the British Parliament in large measure, to look upon their own legislatures as taking its place in their life, and to view the crown, from which had issued their charters and privileges, as the connecting bond between them and the home government. When, therefore, the attempt was made to revive some of the lost authority of Parliament, under Grenville in 1763, it met first with remonstrance, then with opposition, and later with revolution. But the authority of the crown, even though it might be thought to be abused, was not seriously questioned. The limits to it, it was assumed, had been set by the Revolution of 1688, and it was only when these were believed to have been exceeded that the final stage of opposition to what was regarded as the unconstitutional aggression of the crown, was entered upon.

In this contest the theories of the origin and end of government, and the relations of the colonies to Great Britain were threshed over to such an extent that every thinking man knew the value of the grain winnowed out. Otis, the Adamses, Stephen Hopkins, Daniel Dulany, Richard Bland, Dickinson, Wilson, Hamilton, and Jefferson, to mention only the more important, all lent a helping hand. And though they differed in details and occasionally in results, they were in substantial agreement upon the following points. Before the time of the institution of government men were in a state of nature, and in possession of certain natural rights, life, liberty and property, which are antecedent to all rights acquired under government, and hence transcend them. In this state each man is perfectly free and independent, and no man is born ruler of others, but all are created free and equal in the right to rule themselves.

As certain inconveniences arise under these conditions, however, men enter into a social contract, by their own consent agreeing to form governments and give up certain of their inherent rights, that they may thereby ensure others to themselves and to the body politic which they institute, but especially that they may be rendered the more secure in the possession of their property. As their consent is necessary to this action, it follows that none of their property can be taken without this consent, given in person or by representatives chosen for that purpose. Hence " taxation without representation is tyranny." The right to representation, and of determination as to the disposal of property, was not one derived from the British constitution, but is one of the inherent rights of man which no authority can take away. Taxation without representation was slavery, taxation with representation was freedom. They had grown accustomed to the latter and would not submit to the former. Underlying the theory of natural rights and of the consent of the governed was the doctrine of popular sovereignty. " That the people are the basis of all legitimate political authority was a proposition which was little disputed at this time. . . . The inherent and inalienable sovereignty of the people was therefore assumed as a political principle of incontestable validity,—a premise which could not be assailed. Although frequent reference was made to this doctrine, there was little attempt at scientific discussion of the idea: it seemed, indeed, to be so generally recognized that elaborate argument upon the question was superfluous."[1] Side by side with these views went that of the sacredness of the right of revolution, which was accepted with no less unanimity than that of popular sovereignty. To defend their property against aggression was not only a right but a duty, and if in that defense governments were overturned, it was but the alternative to submission and slavery.

But brief consideration of this analysis of the views of the Fathers is requisite to discern in how much they breathe the spirit of Locke throughout. By them none was more often quoted, none more frequently appealed to, to justify the rectitude of their convictions. To no writer was he unfamiliar, and his very words were reproduced by many to help make a telling point. And of no one are these statements so true as of Jefferson, to whose metaphysical mind Locke seems to have made an especial appeal. Hooker and Hobbes and Sydney, too, receive their fair share of attention, but in no sense to the same extent as Locke. There was a time, now happily gone forever, when it was the fashion sneeringly to pass by the philosophy of the Declaration with a brief reference to its French origin.

[1] Merriam, *op. cit.*, 53–4.

But this was the result of a superficial confusion
of apparent similarity with derivation. A year
before Rousseau's *Contrat Social* made its appearance, Otis had produced the first of his pamphlets,
and before Rousseau's work was known in this
country, had issued his *Rights of the Colonists
Asserted*. These two works, full of the English
political thought of the seventeenth century, were
the direct antecedents to all the polemics of the following years, and contained the substance of the
ideas that grew to be the familiars of the people.
Montesquieu, it is true, was well-known and often
cited in their arguments, but the views he held dis-
tinctly showed the influence of his visit to England
and of the philosophy of Locke. In fact, the doctrine of the separation of powers, upon which Montesquieu laid so much stress, and which is perhaps
the best known of his contributions to political science, is not much more than a reproduction of the
gist of Locke's twelfth chapter. But we search the
American pamphlets of the time in vain for any
references to Rousseau's theories. And why should
they have been resorted to when in their own language their own views were expressed to such good
purpose and effect?

But it would never have been possible to base a
revolution in large measure upon a political philosophy, had the principles of that philosophy not been

so frequently reiterated as to become the common property of the people, and if its application to English history had not been so well understood. The contentions of the colonial leaders of thought were voiced in some sixty pamphlets, to mention only the more important, produced between the years 1761 and 1776. Not one failed to ground its argument as much upon theories of natural right and social compact, as upon rights possessed under the British constitution. This does not take into account the great multitude of contributions that filled the gazettes, from the days of Otis's stand against Writs of Assistance to those of 1776, when discussions favoring and opposing independence crowded the columns of every number of every issue. But this was not all. Petitions and resolutions of colonial assemblies and committees, drawn by the very men who were disseminating their views by means of pamphlets, served but to echo the sentiments of the disputants, making them resound throughout the land. Interpretations of the British constitution and of its relation to the colonies, went side by side with the assumption of natural rights, especially in the earlier stages, as witness the Declaration of Rights of 1774. Therefore, when the time was ripe to state the reasons for it and to declare independence, the popular mind had been well prepared for its reception. Every man knew, or

thought he knew perfectly, what were his rights by
nature as well as those which were his by reason of
his understanding of the British constitution. And
every man knew, or thought he knew, how in the
previous fifteen years these rights had been infringed upon. When the time for independence
came he could therefore be appealed to for support
upon philosophic as well as upon constitutional
grounds, with the full assurance that these appeals
would fall upon welcoming ears.

In stating the case finally, it had to be put upon the
highest plane that the exigencies would allow, to
intermingle with a maximum of fact a modicum of
idealism. The opening paragraphs of the Declaration of Independence represent this idealistic philosophy. Jefferson, practical man that he was, no
more pretended to believe that the ideals which he
was giving voice to were attainable, or were attained, at the time he was writing the Declaration,
than he later believed that the constitution was the
most perfect instrument of government that could
be devised. But this was no reason for not setting
down the current high-minded conceptions of the
origin and end of government. When, therefore,
he wrote of the self-evident truths, " that all men are
created equal, that they are endowed by their Creator with certain inalienable Rights; that among
these are Life, Liberty, and the pursuit of Happi-

ness. That to secure these rights, Governments are instituted among Men, deriving their just powers from the consent of the governed,—That whenever any Form of Government becomes destructive of these ends, it is the Right of the People to alter or abolish it, and to institute new Government, laying its foundation on such principles and organizing its powers in such form, as to them shall seem most likely to effect their Safety and Happiness," he was but giving terse expression to the widely diffused convictions of the period. And in doing this he sought out the best model, and repeated the concepts, often even the very phraseology and arguments, of his master John Locke.[1]

And as Jefferson was stating a political and not a moral philosophy, when he wrote that all men are created equal,[2] he conceived equality in the sense of political equality, which was the general

[1] A reading of Locke's second *Treatise* will show how thoroughly every sentence and expression in it were graven on Jefferson's mind. Note especially paragraphs 4, 54, 220, 222, 225, 230.

[2] No error is more common than to quote this clause " all men are created *free* and equal." In the preparation of his careful summary, Jefferson aimed to include no terms over which controversy might arise unnecessarily. To a slaveholding people the inclusion of the word " free " might have occasioned this. Accordingly we find in his original manuscript draft the words " & independent " following " equal," crossed out.

understanding. Not of equality in every respect, but of equality before the law, in rights, privileges, and legal capacities. Here again he followed Locke, who held, " Though I have said ' that all men by nature are equal,' I cannot be supposed to understand all sorts of ' equality.' Age or virtue may give men a just precedency. Excellency of parts and merit may place others above the common level . . . and yet all this consists with the equality which all men are in respect of jurisdiction or dominion one over another, which was the equality I there spoke of as proper to the business in hand, being that every man hath his natural freedom without being subjected to the will or authority of any other man."[1] And Jefferson in his later life put these theories into practice in his battles for the democracy,[2] as Lincoln did in his fight against slavery.[3]

It is, however, when Jefferson comes to give the reasons for overturning the existing form of government that we find ourselves in the immediate presence of Locke, listening to his very voice. The third and fourth sentences of the second paragraph of the Declaration[4] are, in remarkable phraseology,

[1] Second *Treatise*, § 54.

[2] For Jefferson's later views see *Works*, IX, 425, 426, and Merriam, *op. cit.*, Chapter IV.

[3] *Works*, I, 232.

[4] " Prudence, indeed, will dictate that Governments long established should not be changed for light and transient

THE PHILOSOPHY OF THE DECLARATION 203

an epitome of the salient points of Locke's last chapter. It was necessary to assume the establishment of a tyranny that abolished the freedom which was theirs by natural right, or else there was no justification for a revolution, since government should be dissolved only by reason of the specific usurpations already cited.

The investigation into the adequacy of the facts which Jefferson next proceeds to submit to a candid world, to prove the righteousness of his reasoning, will form the subject of the next chapters. And bound up with these facts are the colonial contentions respecting the constitutional relations between the colonies and the home government, and the rights and privileges to which by their charters they were entitled as free-born English citizens, as announced in the declaration of rights of 1774.

The influence of the Declaration upon our political institutions (or rather the influence of the ideas

causes; and accordingly all experience hath shown, that mankind are more disposed to suffer, while evils are sufferable, than to right themselves by abolishing the forms to which they are accustomed. But when a long train of abuses and usurpations, pursuing invariably the same Object evinces a design to reduce them under absolute Despotism, it is their right, it is their duty, to throw off such Government, and to provide new Guards for their future security. Such has been the patient sufferance of these Colonies, and such is now the necessity which constrains them to alter their former Systems of Government."

of which is was the summary expression) has been profound. The concepts outlined above were the fundamental ideas of the men who were given the task of establishing the plans of government fashioned during and immediately following the revolution. And inasmuch as no small part of their preaching was that the ultimate seat of power was in the people, to the people was given a greater share in the control of government than the world had ever before been witness to.[1] No constitution failed to include the philosophy of the Declaration in some form, though it was not adopted to the same extent by all. It appears in those of Massachusetts and Virginia, in respect of the reasons for instituting governments, and in them all in respect of the looseness of government, since it was held that government was a necessary evil and the less of it there was the better for the happiness of the individual and society. This idea was given its most striking expression in the Articles of Confederation, which soon proved to be but the " rope of sand " its framers designed.

Again, the separation of powers, made familiar by Montesquieu, was characteristic of all, though the legislature, so much exalted by Locke as the

---

[1] See the constitutions of Massachusetts, Virginia, North and South Carolina, and Pennsylvania, in Poore's *Charters and Constitutions.*

exponent of the popular will, was now given as great prominence as Parliament had acquired in England. Coincident to this was the jealousy of the executive, and his power was consequently restricted in many ways, and made practically subordinate to the will of the legislature, the immediate representative of the sovereign people. Further, to render the people as nearly supreme as possible, the frequency of elections was repeatedly insisted on.[1]

But it is not to the constitutions of the period of the revolution alone, that the philosophy of the Declaration has been limited. It has affected the whole fabric of our constitutional and legal development, and to an especial degree in its social compact phases. Notably this was the case at the time of the formation of the constitution, when men thought and spoke constantly of agreement and consent in the terms of the compact philosophy.[2] It has pervaded all our law,[3] so that "in reading Locke we cannot fail to be struck with the resemblance between some of his deductions and the doctrines of our own jurists; and we might almost suppose that the ' Treatises on Government ' were in-

[1] Merriam, *op. cit.,* 74 *et seq.*

[2] See the brilliant article of Professor A. C. McLaughlin in *Am. Hist. Rev.,* Vol. V, 467 *et seq.*

[3] A. L. Lowell, *Essays on Government,* 155–156.

tended to be a commentary on the principles of
American Constitutional Law." And it is only
within comparatively recent times that the judiciary
is beginning to free itself from these concepts, fundamental in the establishment of our political institutions.

The impress made by the theory of natural rights
and the social compact on our political and legal
history has been so deep, that many more years of
development will be required before these ideas can
be completely superseded. And if this is ever successfully done, it will be accomplished by an unconscious rather than by any conscious process. They
furnished the incentive to the revolution, as well as
the argument for the contest against slavery. The
roots of this theory are so deeply imbedded in the
political history of England and America, underlying which is a stratum of the Old Testament teaching derived through the Puritan Revolution, that it
will continue to be popular until that day, when the
Declaration of Independence is no longer taught in
the schools and ceases to be read before admiring
throngs.

Nor can the evolutionary theory of the origin of
government and society, now generally accepted in
some form by teachers of political science, be made
the basis for any such popular uprisings as have
been the outcome of the older philosophy. The lat-

ter is instinct with life and can therefore readily be made to appeal to the emotions of men, through which alone great movements are achieved. The organic philosophy appeals only to man's reason, and as yet only to that of the higher thinkers. Upon such a foundation no great social or political movement ever was nor ever yet can be builded. Future generations will have recourse, in their up-risings, to the old guide, or else will seek a new, as yet not in evidence.

CHAPTER X

(1) The " Facts Submitted to a Candid World "

BEFORE undertaking an explanation of the grievances recited in the Declaration, it may be well to
pass in review the method by which the British government exercised supervision over the colonies.
The commercial policy inaugurated by Charles I in
1645, and extended in the Navigation Act of October, 1651, was continued under Cromwell and his
successors.[1] By December, 1660, the trade of the
American colonies had become of sufficient importance to induce Charles II to put its superintend-
ence and management in the hands of a standing
Council for Trade and Foreign Plantations.[2]

[1] Beer, *Commercial Policy of England toward the American
Colonies,* Columbia College *Studies,* III, No. 2, 29, 37. The
Navigation Acts are in MacDonald, *Select Charters Ill. of
Am. Hist.,* 1606–1775.

[2] Board of Trade Journals, I, fo. 1. The copy of the min-
utes of the Commissioners for Trade and Plantations, cited
in these pages under the caption, " Board of Trade Journals,"
is that recently copied for the Historical Society of Pennsylvania, an exact reproduction, page for page, of the originals.
The statements respecting the various councils and committees, known generally as the Board of Trade, have been procured from the volumes just mentioned, and from *Documents
Relating to the Colonial History of New York,* I, xxviii–
xxix.

Fourteen years later, by reason of political considerations, the commission of the existing council was revoked, and their books and papers were ordered to be delivered to the clerk of the Privy Council.[1] On March 12 of the following year (1675), Charles II, by order in council, referred the affairs, of which the old council had taken cognizance, to a committee of the Privy Council consisting of the Lord Chancellor, Lord Treasurer, Lord Privy Seal, and others, who were to meet once a week and report their proceedings from time to time to the King in council. This arrangement was continued under James II and William III, though the latter gave to the committee the title of Board for Trade and Foreign Plantations. The importance which the trade of the colonies assumed, during the first few years of the reign of the last mentioned monarch, caused him to issue a commission, on May 15, 1696, establishing a permanent organization for this Board. The principal officers of state, including the Keeper of the Great Seal, the President of the Privy Council, and others, were created Commissioners of Trade and Plantations. Virtually without further change, they continued to control colonial affairs until March 11, 1752, when their functions were extended to include the recommendation of persons to fill vacancies in colonial gov-

[1] December 21, 1674.

14

ernorships and other offices, and they were made
practically the sole medium for correspondence with
the colonies. On August 8, 1766, the board, which
had acquired a position of quasi-independence, had
its prerogatives somewhat curtailed by an order in
council requiring that letters of instructions should
be issued to the governors of the colonies directing
them to correspond with the Secretary of State,
sending duplicates to the Board of Trade. On
January 20, 1768, the office of Secretary of State
for the Colonies was instituted, and Hillsborough
became its first incumbent. No further change was
made in the method of carrying on official relations
with the colonies until 1782, when the secretaryship
for the colonies was abolished.

The usual procedure, during the period of the
revolutionary agitation, was for the governors to
transmit reports, the acts passed by the legislatures,
together with the journals of the assemblies and
councils, and any petitions that may have been formulated, to the Board of Trade. By that body they
were given careful consideration, the acts being
referred invariably to the solicitor-general for an
opinion as to their consonance with the laws of England and with the provisions of the colonial charters.
His report was usually final, and recommendations
by the Board respecting the allowance or disallowance of acts of the colonial legislatures, in the latter

case accompanied by the reasons therefor, with suggestions for amendment or alteration, were transmitted to the King in council. The King in conjunction with the Lords of the Committee of Council for Plantation Affairs made the final disposition, and the results were transmitted to the colonial governors, in the earlier period by the Board of Trade, and later by the Secretary for the Colonies.

This elaborate machinery for the supervision of colonial affairs worked sometimes with considerable smoothness, at others with great difficulty, for the control thus exercised was far from being nominal in character. The proceedings in the colonies were often given minute examination, and the royal prerogative of disallowing a colonial act was put in practice on frequent occasions. In reaching their determinations the Board was aided by the agents whom practically all the colonies maintained in London to look after their affairs. These agents, among whom Franklin and Burke were the most noted, often represented several colonies, and appeared before the Board whenever they could thereby advance the interests of the colonies. At times they were given hearings extending over a number of sessions. But the process of transmitting all laws to England was a tedious requirement occasioning much delay, was a never-ending source of irritation to the colonies, and caused them to resort to various subterfuges to circumvent it.

The deeds that led directly to the revolution are easy to discover, as they lie upon the surface of events, and are not readily to be overlooked. But beneath these were more deep-seated causes, that may be said to have taken their origin with the founding of the colonies. The Navigation Acts aimed to control the colonial commerce for the benefit of England. By restrictions on such colonial manufactures as woolens, hats, and the products of iron, it was intended to make the colonies "the vent of England's manufactures."[1] The bounties granted for the production of naval stores and related products, and the later concessions designed to render submission to taxation by Parliament palatable, were by no means a compensation, either in degree or in kind, for the unwelcome restrictions.[2] As long as the colonies were in their infancy they stood in need of the tutelage of the home government. As they grew to manhood they found it possible to stand by themselves, were able in most respects to safeguard their own welfare. During this period of development, and largely aiding in it, control by the British authorities was most lax. At the very time when the fostering care of the home government came no longer to be required, the turn in the tide of the British colonial

[1] Beer, *op. cit.*, 66.
[2] *Ibid., passim.*

policy set in under Grenville. Close supervision then succeeded gross neglect. It was as if a parent had allowed his offspring to attain majority without any serious attempt at influencing the formation of his character, and then suddenly undertook to enforce the authority that had been kept so long in abeyance.

Again, just when this stage of development was reached, the requirement that all laws be sent to England for revision, and for allowance or disallowance, proved most irksome and worked inevitably towards disunion. The exercise of close supervision over practically every colonial enactment, though recognized as a perfectly legal exaction, was one that readily gave rise to many abuses and much controversy.

It was not without reason, therefore, that emphasis was put upon this serious grievance in the Declaration, that it was given the position of honor in the opening paragraphs, and that in the first two charges against the King,[1] Jefferson leaps at once into the thick of the controversy. In the terse words of these two grievances he has included the

[1] " He has refused his Assent to Laws, the most wholesome and necessary for the public good."

" He has forbidden his Governors to pass Laws of immediate and pressing importance, unless suspended in their operation till his Assent should be obtained ; and when so suspended has utterly neglected to attend to them."

whole of the great question of the constitutional relations of the colonies to the crown, that agitated England and America for all of a century.

Excepting only Rhode Island, Connecticut, and Maryland, all the colonies had fully experienced what it meant to enact laws " wholesome and neces- sary for the public good," only to have them re- peatedly rejected by the King in council. In addi- tion, the royal governors were often specifically instructed to withhold assent from certain kinds of legislation. Every man had felt the strong arm of the home government interfering, not only in the public, but in his private affairs as well. To such an extent had this been carried, that after 1773 not even a divorce could be granted in any of the col- onies, for the penalty was instant dismissal to the governor who gave countenance to such a law. That same year witnessed at least twenty important colonial laws rejected by the King upon various pre- texts.[1] The leading men in America were keenly alive to the irritating effects of this course, and Jefferson had already given expression to the feel- ing existing, when he wrote, in 1774, " for the most trifling reasons, and sometimes for no conceivable reason at all, his majesty has rejected laws of the most salutary tendency."[2] What Jefferson had in

[1] *Board of Trade Journal,* 1773.

[2] *Works,* I, 440.

mind, however, was the repeated disallowance of certain laws passed by the colonies to promote their welfare, but which came into conflict with the policy of the home authorities. Such were the laws of Virginia, and other Southern colonies, designed to prohibit the slave-trade and the introduction of convicts, and those of nearly all the colonies for issuing bills of credit and for naturalizing aliens. Massachusetts, as is well known, had her great disputes over laws relating to the question of compensating, in her own way, the sufferers from the Stamp Act riots, as well as over methods of taxation and the appropriation of money for salaries of government officials.

Steps to restrict the importation of slaves were taken at an early date, but every law of this nature was disallowed by the crown, on the ground that an important branch of British trade would thereby be interfered with.[1] Thus fared the acts framed in South Carolina in 1760, in New Jersey in 1763, and in Virginia in 1772. The rejection of Virginia's law caused particular irritation, since it was the latest in a long series of similar ineffectual acts, and had been accompanied by an especial appeal to the King that the governor might be allowed to assent to it. A royal instruction was issued to the governor of New Hampshire, upon his appointment in

[1] Dubois, *Suppression of the Slave Trade*.

1761, preventing him from signing any law imposing duties on negroes imported into that colony, and
subsequent royal instructions required the colonists
to desist from their opposition to the slave-trade.
The strength of feeling on this subject is exhibited
in the stand taken by the Congress of 1774, which
by the Articles of Association prohibited the importation of slaves, and the slave-trade after December
1, of that year. And again, on April 6, 1776, when
the ports of the country were thrown open to trade
with the world, the only qualification was the resolve to import no slaves into any of the colonies.

The attempts to prevent the entrance of convicts,
regarded, if possible, with even less favor than
slaves, met with no greater success. Many of this
class, under the English law which allowed those
convicted of crime the option, in some cases, between
imprisonment, death, or transportation to America,
preferred to leave England. Their arrival met
with opposition, particularly in Virginia, Maryland
and Pennsylvania, which colonies endeavored by
laws passed early in their history, to restrict the
entrance of this undesirable class. But every such
act was disallowed. Franklin spoke of this in
1768 as having " long been a great grievance to the
plantations in general,"[1] and John Dickinson wrote
in the same year, " the emptying their jails upon

---

[1] *Works,* Sparks' ed., II, 496, IV, 252.

us and making the Colonies a Receptacle for the Rogues and Villains: an Insult and Indignity not to be thought of, much less borne without Indignation and Resentment."[1]

Also, owing to the scarcity of specie, bills of credit were then an absolute necessity in order that the colonists might be enabled to carry on trade by means other than those of mere barter. But the policy of King and Parliament was against the allowance of any issues of paper money. First came the breaking up of the Massachusetts and Pennsylvania land bank schemes,[2] by an act of Parliament in 1751, which restrained the northern colonies from making any new issues or reissuing old bills, except in sudden emergencies. Then in September, 1764, basing its action on a report of Lord Hillsborough, president of the Board of Trade, Parliament passed an act prohibiting any issues of bills of credit from being made legal tender, and placing restrictions upon them in other respects. Frequent petitions against this act effected no result.[3] In 1765, when Governor Moore was sent to New York, he received a royal instruction to assent to no law whatever for striking bills of credit, though this was modified

[1] Almon's *Prior Docs.*, 224. *Life and Writings of Dickinson*, II, 413. Address of Philadelphia Merchants, April 25, 1768.

[2] Shepherd, *Penna. under Proprietary Govt.*, 422.

[3] Franklin's *Works*, VII, 429–430.

somewhat in the following year when permission
was granted to issue bills under certain restrictions,
and if not in contravention of the act of 1764.
Laws of New Jersey[1] (1758 and 1769), of Pennsylvania (1759), and of New York (1769 and
1770)[2] for issuing these bills were disallowed by the
King in spite of urgent petitions in their favor.

When Massachusetts, in 1766, compensated those
who suffered from the riots occasioned by the attempted enforcement of the Stamp Act, pardoning
the offenders at the same time, the law was
promptly disallowed. Not only this, but the King
by order in council, May 13, 1767, required the governor to have a law passed compensating the sufferers, " unmixed with any other matter whatsoever."[3] A few years later, when the controversy
thickened, the Governor of Massachusetts and the
Assembly of that colony were continually at logger-
heads. The disallowance by the former of the bill
passed in 1771,[4] taxing the new Customs Commissioners, created by the Townshend Act, served not
only to increase the existing feeling of irritation at
having such a body of foreign and uncontrolled
officers in their midst, but also tended to interfere

[1] *N. J. Archives,* 1st ser., X, 115.

[2] *Docs. Rel. Col. Hist. of N. Y.,* VIII, 202–205, 215.

[3] Almon's *Prior Docs.,* 141–142; *Mass. Hist. Coll.,* 6th
Series, IX, 82 *et seq.*

[4] *Mass. State Papers,* 306–307.

seriously with the necessary legislation of the colony. The disallowance of naturalization laws need not detain us here, for we shall have occasion to speak of them below.

Passing to the second charge, we find it but a refinement, or rather an elaboration, of the preceding. The first intimation that a closer control over colonial legislation was intended, came when Parliament addressed the King, in 1740,[1] requesting that governors of the colonies be instructed to assent to no law that failed to contain a clause suspending its action until transmitted to England for consideration. This was followed by a royal instruction of March, 1752, requiring a revision of the laws in force in all the royal provinces, and ordering at the same time their transmission to England, and the insertion in each of a clause " suspending and deferring the execution thereof until the royal will and pleasure may be known thereon."[2] A case in point arose in New York, in 1759, when Governor De Lancey was instructed to assent to no law empowering justices of the peace to try minor causes, unless such act contained the suspending clause.[3] The endeavor to suppress lotteries, then so great a factor

---

[1] *Answer to the Declaration of Independence,* 5th ed., London, 1776, p. 21. *Commons Journal,* XXIII, 528.

[2] *Docs. Rel. Col. Hist. N. Y.,* VI, 755-756.

[3] *Ibid.,* VII, 406.

in the economic and social life of the colonies, was a stroke of policy that made its effects felt seriously in all the colonies. Down to 1769 they flourished unrestricted, but in June of that year the royal governors were enjoined from assenting to any law creating them that lacked the suspending clause,—a practical veto upon all attempts at raising funds by such means.[1] Special instructions (1771) prohibited Governor Martin of Virginia from signing any law of this character, on the reasonable ground that the practice " doth tend to disengage those who become adventurers therein from that spirit of industry and attention to their proper callings and occupations on which the public welfare so greatly depends."[2]

As respects the latter portion of this second charge,—the neglect of laws suspended in their action until the royal assent was obtained,—we have a typical instance in four laws passed in Virginia, in 1770, and transmitted to England at once. They were not even considered by the Lords Commissioners for Trade and Plantations until nearly three years after their enactment.[3] Three were then confirmed, but a fourth was set aside for final action at a later date, until more information respecting it

[1] *Ibid.*, VIII, 174-175.
[2] *N. C. Col. Recs.*, VIII, 515.
[3] *Board of Trade Journal*, 1773, Vol. 81, 49-50.

could be obtained from the governor of Virginia. Jefferson gave expression to the feeling in Virginia when he wrote, in 1774, " his Majesty permitted our laws to lie neglected in England for years, neither confirming them by his assent, nor annulling them by his negative; so that such of them as suspend themselves until his majesty's assent be obtained, we have feared, might be called into existence at some future and distant period, when the time and change of circumstances shall have rendered them destructive to his people here. . . . his majesty by his instruction has laid his governors under such restrictions that they can pass no law of any moment unless it have such suspending clause; so that, however immediate may be the call for legislative interposition, the law cannot be executed until it has twice crossed the Atlantic, by which time the evil may have spent its whole force."[1]

Closely related to this grievance was the opposition created by the increase, after 1770, in the number of royal instructions issued to the governors. Every royal governor, moreover, upon setting out for his post, was furnished with instructions by which he was to be guided in the conduct of his office. New policies were frequently initiated in this way, and gave rise to many clashes between the governors and the legislatures. The veto power of

[1] *Summary View, Works,* I, 440–441.

the governor, under his instructions, was always a source of irritation, and was looked upon as an infringement upon the legislative independence of the assemblies.[1] So far as regards Massachusetts, Samuel Adams contended that instructions were given the force of laws, and thus came to be subversive of charter privileges.[2] And Pownall held that " in some cases of emergency, and in the cases of the concerns of individuals, the instruction has been submitted to, but the principle never."[3]

With the third charge,[4] however, we reach the first grievance in the list that meant much to the men of the days of the revolution, but which conveys no message to us. It has to do with the erection of additional counties out of newly-settled districts, and with their representation in the colonial assemblies. As the population spread out from the centers into the more remote regions, the inhabitants demanded representation in the legislatures. The colonists claimed this power as a right. But the crown, in accordance with the English law, regarded the issuance of writs for representation as a preroga-

[1] Greene, *The Provincial Governor,* 162–163.

[2] *Mass. State Papers,* 307.

[3] *Administration of the Colonies,* 39.

[4] " He has refused to pass other Laws for the accommodation of large districts of people, unless those people would relinquish the right of Representation in the Legislature, a right inestimable to them and formidable to tyrants only."

tive of the sovereign, to be exercised in the colonies
through the royal governors. Holding such conflicting views, clashes were inevitable. They came
in New Hampshire, New York, New Jersey, and Virginia, the colonies most actively engaged in peo-
pling their western lands. New York tried to give
representation to two newly erected counties, Cum-
berland[1] (1766) and Albany (1768), but was prevented in each case. More than that, in the latter
instance the King graciously consented to the division of the county and the election of two members
from it to the Assembly, but only on condition that
in the law establishing the new county no mention
should be made of representation.[2] The year 1767
witnessed the issuance of a royal instruction em-
bodying, in most stringent form, the design to control absolutely the whole matter of representation
in the assemblies, and the qualifications of electors
and the elected as well.[3] Virginia felt this bore with
particular severity upon her, and her leading men
knew well that Governor Martin had, in 1771, received explicit orders to carry out this instruction to
the letter. Jefferson regarded it as a great grievance and an infringement on the rights of freemen.

[1] *Docs. Rel. Col. Hist. of N. Y.*, VII, 918. *Journal of N.
Y. Legislative Council*, II, 1594–1596.
[2] *Docs. Rel. Col. Hist. of N. Y.*, VIII, 100.
[3] *Ibid.*, 946.

According to his view, the people living on the western borders and having no local courts, nor any local government, found the administration of justice almost an impossibility. " Does his Majesty seriously wish," wrote he, " and publish it to the world, that his subjects should give up the glorious right of representation, with all the benefits derived from that, and submit themselves the absolute slaves of his sovereign will?"[1]

In New Hampshire the dispute was of early origin, and resulted for a time in the defeat of the contention of the assembly which aimed to give to that body the control over representation. But in the last days of the old order the controversy was revived, when rights of various kinds were being examined with careful scrutiny and were being asserted with vigor, if not always with discretion. Upon this very point, of the admission of new members from the towns of Plymouth, Orford, and Lime, " called in " by the King's writ by Governor Wentworth, the assembly made its final stand, and it breathed its last breath, on July 18, 1775, with this contention on its lips.[2]

We come next to the three charges[3] respecting the

[1] *Works*, I, 441.

[2] *Force*, 4th, II, 1175, 1678–1679. The reply of Governor Wentworth to the claims of the Assembly is an able document, and thoroughly sound in its reasoning.

[3] " He has called together legislative bodies at places unusual, uncomfortable, and distant from the depository of their

removal of assemblies, their dissolution, and the failure to convoke them after long periods. These need detain us but a moment, since the details of the removal of the Massachusetts Assembly to Cambridge[1] and Salem,[2] and that of South Carolina to Beaufort,[3] are many and varied, and are to be found in all histories of the times. Moreover, all accounts tell of the dissolution of the Virginia Assembly, in 1765, after the passage of Patrick Henry's famous resolutions; of that of Massachusetts, in 1768, for refusing to review the action on the Circular Letter; and of those of South Carolina and Georgia for daring to withstand Lord Hillsborough's order to treat that letter " with the contempt it deserves." In like manner, the passage of the ringing Virginia Resolves, in May, 1769, against the revival of the statute of Henry VIII, permitting of the transporta-

public Records, for the sole purpose of fatiguing them into compliance with his measures."

" He has dissolved Representative Houses repeatedly, for opposing with manly firmness his invasions on the rights of the people."

" He has refused for a long time, after such dissolutions, to cause others to be elected; whereby the Legislative powers, incapable of Annihilation, have returned to the People at large for their exercise; the State remaining in the mean time exposed to all the dangers from invasion from without, and convulsions within."

[1] 1769–1772.

[2] 1774.

[3] 1772.

15

tion to England for trial of persons accused of treason, led to another dissolution.   And when a Continental Congress was being called together, in 1774, all but three of the colonies had to elect delegates by means of provincial conventions or committees of correspondence, because their assemblies had been dissolved by the governors.   The last of the charges relates undoubtedly to the calling of the Boston town meeting of September, 1768, to urge upon the governor the necessity for convening the Assembly, which had been dissolved because of its action on the Circular Letter, while troops, but recently ordered to Boston to quell the disturbances there, " exposed the citizens to all the dangers of invasion from without and convulsions from within."   And in New Hampshire, South Carolina, and Virginia, in the autumn of 1775, affairs of government had come to such a pass that an appeal to the Congress was made for advice.   The answer came to establish governments that will " best promote the happiness of the people," and " most effectually secure peace and good order."[1]

We turn now from the familiar details of dissolved assemblies to the little known affairs of land grants and naturalization.[2]   The proclamation of

[1] See p. 34.

[2] " He has endeavored to prevent the population of these States ; for that purpose obstructing the Laws of Naturaliza-

the autumn of 1763,[1] in which the King expressed his intention to erect new colonies out of lands that the colonists claimed by right of charter, meant the serious curtailment of these claims and the obstruction of the migration westward, and marked the initiation of a new policy. It restricted the limits of the colonies claiming rights to the South Seas to " the heads or sources of any of the rivers which fall into the Atlantic Ocean." Beyond the " heads or sources " was a reserved domain, out of which the governors were prohibited from making any grants whatever. Worse still, those who had settled in these regions were peremptorily ordered to vacate, on the pretext that the lands were reserved for the Indians. But the movement had already set toward the west, and no such restrictions could check it. Land companies, in which Franklin and men of his stamp were interested, made petition for the right to found colonies, but met only with refusal. Yet the westward migration could not be stayed, although this was attempted by means of an Order in Council of 1773,[2] prohibiting the royal governors from issuing any patents until further instructions

tion of Foreigners ; refusing to pass others to encourage their migrations hither, and raising the conditions of new Appropriations of Lands."

[1] MacDonald, *Sel. Charters, 1606–1775*, 267.

[2] April 7, 1773. *N. C. Col. Recs.,* IX, 632–3.

were given. These followed a year later,[1] and were even more grievous, in that they raised the "conditions of new appropriations of lands." The royal lands were to be sold at specified times to the highest bidders, at the upset price of sixpence per acre, and with the reservation of an annual quit-rent of one half-penny an acre to the King. No lands were to be disposed of except in this way. Jefferson had this in mind when he wrote the Declaration, and when he said, in 1774, "His Majesty has lately taken on him to advance the terms of purchase, and of holding to the double of what they were, by which means the acquisition of lands being rendered difficult, the population of our country is likely to be checked."[2] Only the advance of the revolution prevented the carrying out of these provisions, which were everywhere regarded as harsh and unjust.

Closely allied to the question of granting lands was that of the naturalization of aliens. This was very generally practiced by the colonies, not so much with a view to conferring political rights as for the purpose of attracting desirable immigrants to open up their undeveloped territory. Where the right to transmit his property to posterity was accorded him,

[1] February 3, 1774. *Docs. Rel. Col. Hist. N. Y.*, VIII, 410–412.

[2] *Works*, I, 444. See also on "raising the conditions of new Appropriations of lands," *ibid.*, 452–453.

there would the immigrant settle. Such acts of naturalization met with no comment from the home government till the proclamation of 1763 was issued. From that time on, however, few of these acts passed the ordeal of the Commissioners for Trade and Plantations without recommendation for disallowance. Finally, in November, 1773, came the royal instruction prohibiting absolutely the naturalization of any aliens, and the passage of any acts to that end. It was a heavy blow to the prosperity of the larger land-holding colonies, Virginia, New York, New Jersey, and Pennsylvania, the settlement of which bade fair now to be seriously interfered with.

That part of the same charge mentioning the refusal to assent to laws encouraging immigration, has reference to an act passed in North Carolina in 1771. It exempted persons coming immediately from Europe from all forms of taxation for four years. It was disallowed, however, by the King, in February, 1772, on the ground that it related especially to certain Scotch immigrants, since its provisions applied only to persons coming immediately from Europe, and thus might have an evil effect upon the " landed Interests and Manufacturers of Great Britain and Ireland."[1]

[1] *N. C. Col. Recs.*, IX, 251–252.

We come next to the complaint of the interference with the administration of justice by the refusal
of assent to laws for establishing judiciary powers.[1]
The man whose mind evolved the Declaration knew
that in such a state paper the most crying wrongs of
each colony must, in some measure, be enumerated.
Though it would be best, for the most part, to confine the charges to those restrictive measures that
concerned all alike, the most serious local grievances
of each colony must not be disregarded. The colony whose cause is here advocated is North Carolina.
And unquestionably the political consideration that
she had been the earliest to declare in favor of independence, was the occasion for this signal recognition of her wrongs. Beyond the pages of local histories we seek in vain for the explanation of this
important episode in her history, even though it attained a prominence so great as to find a place in the
Declaration.

The controversy held in mind by Jefferson was an
old one, and began when, in January, 1768, Governor
Tyron signed a law, passed at a previous session
of the Assembly of North Carolina, providing,
among other things, for establishing superior courts
of justice. The law was to be in force for five
years only, and from then to the end of the next

[1] " He has obstructed the Administration of Justice, by refusing his Assent to Laws for establishing Judiciary powers."

regular session of the Assembly   For three years all went well, because the Lords Commissioners for Trade and Plantations paid little attention, in the interval, to colonial laws. Fault was then found with this " superior court act," because of a clause that made the property of persons who had never been in the colony liable to attachment on the suit of the creditor. This was in contravention of the letter and the spirit of the laws of England. Though the Lords Commissioners considered it a serious departure from legal form, they agreed, nevertheless, that if the Assembly would amend the act in this particular, they would not recommend its disallowance.[2] No action, in response to this hint, was taken by the North Carolina Assembly, and after waiting a due season—about a year,—the King issued an instruction prohibiting his governor from giving assent to any law containing the attachment clause, unless it included a provision suspending its operation until the royal pleasure was made known.[3] This had come in February, 1772, and was well timed, for the law was to expire by limitation the next year, and, consequently, if proper provision were not made by the Assembly, no superior courts

[1] Iredell's *N. C. Laws,* Edenton, 1791, 231. *N. C. Col. Recs.,*
VII, 551, 557, 573, 580, 588, 610, 623, 693, 921, No. 5.
[2] *Ibid.,* VIII, 264–267.
[3] *Ibid.,* IX, 235.

would exist in the province. In February, 1773, therefore, when the Assembly passed a new court act, making provision for superior and inferior courts and retaining the objectionable attachment clause, the contest was on in bitter earnest. The first law enacted contained no suspending clause. This the governor, Martin, vetoed.[1] Then the Assembly yielded so far as to add the suspending clause, but retained the attachment provision. Though signed by the governor, it was, of course, disallowed by the King, and meanwhile, as there were no courts in the province, the governor was instructed to establish them on his own responsibility. This he did, but the Assembly refused to recognize his authority, and made no appropriation for the salaries of the judges. Persisting in their determination to have the kind of bill they wanted and to control their own affairs, they passed the one previously disallowed, when they convened again in March, 1774. They were then prorogued for their obstinacy, and practically did not sit again while North Carolina was under British rule. Thus, as a result of the controversy, not only was the Assembly dissolved, because it failed to do as it was bid, but from 1773 until North Carolina assumed State gov-

---

[1] March 6, 1773. *Ibid.*, 583. See also Raper's *North Carolina*, 157–158.

ernment in 1776, there were no courts in the province.[1]

Our first thought, in endeavoring to account for the next charge,[2] is likely to be of the long-standing controversies in New York and Massachusetts over the payment of the salaries of the judiciary, and the conditions of their tenure of office. The question at issue, in both instances, hinged upon granting salaries by colonial appropriation, or permitting payment to be made by the crown. The policy, adopted by Great Britain at an early date (1761), was to refuse to permit judges to hold office during good behavior, as in England, and to insist, instead, that they hold only during the King's pleasure. Made to yield, with no good will, to this enforcement of the royal prerogative, the colonists resisted to the utmost the extension that made it possible to enforce obnoxious laws and decrees by the whole power of a judiciary dependent, not only for its tenure, but for its stipends as well, upon the abso-

---

[1] *N. C. Col. Recs.*, IX, xxvi. There were contests in South Carolina also, in respect of the erection of courts, but they were of minor importance to those in North Carolina. See McCrady, *S. C. under Royal Government*, 628; and *S. C. in the Revolution*, 120–121; Smith, *S. C. as a Royal Prov.*, 134 *et seq.*

[2] " He has made Judges dependent on his Will alone, for the tenure of their offices, and the amount and payment of their salaries."

lute good will of the crown.   The term of tenure
established, to fix salaries was but a repressive step
in advance, although the question did not develop
till 1767.   Then that ill-advised Townshend Act,
known colloquially as the "glass, lead, and paint
act," passed Parliament, and became the law of the
realm.[1]   The preamble stated boldly its design of
raising a revenue to make "a more certain and adequate Provision for defraying the Charge of the
Administration of Justice and the Support of Civil
Government, in such Provinces where it shall be
found necessary."   A paragraph in the bill, ex-
plaining how this was to be carried out, showed that
it was no idle declaration of intention merely.   To
the inhabitants of the colonies, already goaded
nearly to the point of rebellion because of excessive
control of their internal affairs, this meant an intol-
erable interference with their rights, and was not to
be borne.   The colonial contention was that inasmuch as judges held office during the King's pleasure, if they also received their salaries from any
other source than the people to whom they were to
dispense justice, all control over them would be lost,
and no redress could be had, when corruption and
incompetence displaced integrity and learning.

Furthermore, the extension of the jurisdiction of

[1] June 29, 1767.   7 Geo. III, c. 46.   The act is in Mac-
Donald, *Select Charters*, 323.

the admiralty courts, in 1764 and 1768,[1] with great enlargement of their powers, foreshadowed, it was thought, the possible extinction of trial by jury in civil as well as in maritime causes.[2]   The judges of these courts were royal appointees receiving their salaries, supposedly, from fines and the proceeds of the sale of condemned vessels; but, as this source failed to bring in any revenue, they were paid directly out of the royal exchequer.

The greatest of the controversies over judicial salaries, however, is the famous one begun in Massachusetts on that evil day in February, 1773, when Governor Hutchinson announced to the Assembly of the province that the King had made provision for the justices of the superior court, and that consequently no appropriation was necessary for their maintenance.[3]   The Assembly voiced their opposition in vigorous terms, at first in letters of remonstrance and finally in the well known resolutions of March 3, 1773.[4]   And reference was made to this grievance in the Declaration of Rights and the ad-

[1] See Address to Colonies, Oct. 21, 1774, *Journal of Congress.*

[2] The 41st paragraph of the Sugar Act of 1764 (4 Geo. III, c. 15) contained the provisions for enforcing the act, and the recourse to admiralty courts. A part of the act is in MacDonald, *op. cit.,* 273 *et seq.;* the full text in *Statutes at Large,* XXVI, 33–52.

[3] *Mass. State Papers,* 365.

[4] *Ibid.,* 396.

dress to the colonies of 1774, and redress demanded.[1]

From the controversy over judges to that over commissioners for the enforcement of customs laws is but a step. Their appointment is made the basis of the grievance charging that a multitude of new officers had been sent to America "to harass the people and eat out their substance."[2] For, combined with the decision of Townshend to pass an act of taxation, was the determination to enforce it at all hazards. As there was no governmental machinery in America through which to act, a new engine of oppression was instituted by the first of the Townshend Acts.[3] Its provisions were exceedingly modest in that the King was simply authorized to appoint commissioners of customs to reside in America, with power and jurisdiction similar to the British commissioners. They in turn were empowered to appoint an indefinite number of deputies, and it was this multiplication of officers that aroused the hostility of the colonists. Their salaries, moreover, were to be paid out of the receipts from the customs, and constituted the most serious aggres-

[1] *Journal of Congress,* Oct. 14, 1774.

[2] " He has erected a multitude of New Offices, and sent hither swarms of Officers to harrass our people, and eat out their substance."

[3] June 29, 1767. The act is cited as 7 Geo. III, c. 41, and is in MacDonald, *op. cit.,* 321.

sion of this nature to which the colonists took exception.

But little less irritation was caused by the policy initiated by Grenville, in 1764, when he determined upon rigorously enforcing the existing trade laws with a view to putting an end to smuggling. In accordance with this intention, he placed Admiral Colville, naval commander-in-chief on the coasts of North America, virtually at the head of the revenue service. And each captain of a vessel was instructed to take the customs house oath, and aid in the seizure of those engaged in the illicit trade which had been connived at for years.[1] Further, as offences against the revenue act were to be tried in courts of admiralty or vice-admiralty, their increase with new officers became necessary. The first of the new courts with previously unheard-of jurisdiction was opened at Halifax, in 1764, and the act of 1768 made provision for their extension throughout the other colonies.

The next charge has to do with the maintenance of troops in the colonies without the consent of the legislatures.[2] To this may be joined that in which complaint is made of rendering the military independent of and superior to the civil power,[3] as also

[1] Bancroft, original ed., V, 160–162.
[2] " He has kept among us in times of peace, Standing Armies without the Consent of our legislatures."
[3] " He has affected to render the Military independent of and superior to the Civil power."

the later accusation of quartering troops upon the
people.[1] After the peace of 1763, the troops that
had been sent over were not withdrawn and provision had to be made for their support. This was
done by the extension of the provisions of the recently passed Mutiny Act to the American colonies,
in a separate act known as the " Quartering Act."[2]
After the Stamp Act riots several companies of
royal artillery reached Boston in the autumn of
1766, and were quartered at the expense of the
province, by order of Governor Bradford and the
Council. Against this the Assembly remonstrated
on the ground that they alone had the right to make
appropriations for this purpose.[3] In 1768, as
trouble was anticipated over the enforcement of the
Townshend Acts, large increases of troops were
sent to Boston, New York, and elsewhere, and in
each case gave rise to controversy about provision
for their maintenance. The clash at Boston, in
March, 1770, known as the " Boston Massacre," was
the culminating event of this dispute.

The appointment of General Gage as governor
of Massachusetts in 1774, under the Massachusetts
Government Act,[4] making him at the same time

[1] " For Quartering large bodies of armed troops among us."
[2] April, 1765. The provisions of this act are in MacDonald,
op. cit., 306. The act is cited as 5 Geo. III, c. 33.
[3] Winsor, *Narr. and Crit. Hist.*, VI, 38. *Mass. State
Papers*, 105–108.
[4] 14 Geo. III, c. 45. MacDonald, *op. cit.*, 343.

commander-in-chief of the troops in America and the supreme executive authority in the colony, was a combination of the military with the civil jurisdiction which aroused stern opposition throughout the colonies, as rendering " the Military independent of and superior to the Civil power." All of these acts were remonstrated against in the Declaration of Rights and the address to the colonies of 1774. With the accusation last referred to we come to the end of the first division of grievances.

CHAPTER XI

(2) "THE FACTS SUBMITTED TO A CANDID WORLD"

THE master mind of Jefferson perceived that for rhetorical effect he must adopt a manner sufficiently emphatic to inspire enthusiasm, and yet not weary with a long recital of "abuses and usurpations," recounted in the same monotonous style. Therefore, the form of indictment now undergoes a change for a few brief paragraphs. The King alone is now not held solely responsible, but is accused of combining "with others to subject us to a jurisdiction foreign to our constitution, and unacknowledged by our laws: giving his Assent to their Acts of pretended Legislation,"—in part, the very words used by Jefferson two years before.[1] Though Parliament is thus made to bear a share of the burden, it is nowhere mentioned by name, and the principal weight is still put upon the shoulders of the King.

Of the first of the new order of grievances we have already spoken sufficiently.[2] The next, however, which complains of soldiers escaping by mock trials from the consequences of any murders that

[1] *Works*, I, 439.
[2] "For Quartering large bodies of armed troops among us."

they might commit, needs further comment.[1] It
can refer to no other law than that known generally
as the act " for the impartial administration of justice," which passed Parliament on May 20, 1774.[2]
This was one of the acts repeatedly decried in the
state papers of the earlier Congress,[3] and moved
Jefferson to denounce those who would submit to
the enforcement of its provisions as " cowards who
would suffer a countryman to be torn from the
bowels of their society, in order to be thus offered
a sacrifice to parliamentary tyranny," meriting
" that everlasting infamy now fixed on the authors
of the act!"[4]   The act had been passed to provide
for such contingencies as had arisen after the " Boston Massacre "—the trial of persons accused of
murder while in the discharge of their official duties.
By its terms those in His Majesty's service, military as well as civil, accused of murder committed
while executing the laws of the realm in Massachusetts, might obtain a change of venue to some other
province, or to Great Britain, " if it shall appear,

---

[1] " For protecting them, by a mock Trial, from punishment
for any Murders which they should commit on the Inhabitants of these States."

[2] 14 Geo. III, c. 39. MacDonald, *op. cit.*, 351. See also
Answer to the Declaration of Independence, 5th ed., London,
1776, 60, 62.

[3] Declaration of Rights. Address to the Colonies.

[4] *Works*, I, 439.

16

242 THE DECLARATION OF INDEPENDENCE

to the satisfaction of the . . . governor, . . . that an indifferent trial cannot be had within the said province." Provision was made also for the transportation of witnesses as well, and, most grievous of all, the accused might be admitted to bail upon the order of the governor, it mattered not how flagrant the crime charged against him. As there was little likelihood that a British official, military or civil, would be brought to trial in England for committing the crime of executing the law in America, this was regarded as an unwarrantable invasion of colonial rights.

Having thus far dealt in the main with the political side of the grievances, Jefferson, in order that nothing of importance may be omitted, now turns to those oppressions that bore most heavily upon the economic life of the people. And if there be a weakness in the Declaration, it is the failure to dwell to any extent upon the narrow British economic policy toward the colonies, which meant using them for the benefit of the manufacturers and traders at home. In the beginning, as has been noted,[1] the opposition to the enforcement of trade laws, restrictions upon manufactures, and the right to taxation, was based as largely upon economic as upon political grounds. But the material economic grievances were soon lost to view in the eloquent

[1] See p. 7.

maintenance of the right to political liberty that resounded through the land.   Yet Jefferson had devoted no small part of his *Summary View*[1] to a
consideration of the burdens put by law upon the
commerce and manufactures of the colonies, in the
interests of the British merchants.

To cut off the trade of the colonists with all parts
of the world except Great Britain, as written in the
Declaration,[2] was a policy first adopted in the days
of Charles I and Cromwell, and persisted in to the
end.   But the particularly serious acts of aggression were those instituted by Grenville, in 1764,
when he revived the Molasses Act of 1733, by which
an end was intended to be put to the rum traffic of
New England, and the rigorous measures already
referred to for enforcing the existing though nearly
obsolete trade laws.   An idea of the full meaning
of the last intention may be gathered when we
recall that, all in all, about fifty acts had been passed
by Parliament, between 1688 and 1765, for the purpose of binding the colonial trade.   Coming down
to a later day, we have the well-known acts of 1774,
which closed the port of Boston, and the acts of
March, April, and December, 1775,[3] which effectu-

[1] *Works,* I, 434.
[2] " For cutting off our Trade with all parts of the world."
[3] 14 Geo. III, c. 19.   15 Geo. III, c. 10.   16 Geo. III, c. 5.
MacDonald, *op. cit.,* 368, 391.

ally prohibited all trade with the colonies, thereby cutting them off from all the world. The last mentioned act superseded the earlier, was most stringent in its provisions, and punished with confiscation as prizes all vessels caught contravening it.

We come now to the consideration of that clause which has become the chiefest of the familiars of our history—taxation without consent.[1] Reference was here intended to (1) the Sugar Act of 1764, (2) the Stamp Act, (3) the Townshend Acts, and (4) the Tea Acts of 1770 and 1773. By the Sugar Act of 1764, the determination was announced to execute more strictly the trade laws, and, by raising a revenue from the colonies, to help pay off England's debt, more than doubled by the war just concluded. The Molasses Act of 1733,[2] the first of the revenue acts, was aimed to interdict the commerce between the French West Indies and the colonies of the continent, especially New England, and was directly in the interest of the British West Indies which lost in trade, it was claimed, what their French rivals gained. Though in form a revenue act, the duties on rum and spirits, molasses syrup, and sugar imported from the French West Indies to the other colonies, were placed so high as to be prohibitory, and therefore the act worked out in

[1] " For imposing Taxes on us without our Consent."
[2] 6 Geo. II, c. 13. MacDonald, *op. cit.,* 249.

practice merely as a regulation of commerce.[1] Since, however, it was never strictly enforced, its provisions were constantly violated and smuggling was carried on openly. The wind thus sown was reaped in the whirlwind of disregard for laws, except those enacted by colonial legislatures, characteristic of the period of the revolution.

The Sugar Act of 1764[2] revived the Molasses Act, but reduced the duties avowedly for revenue purposes and made it perpetual. Its title began with the words, " an act for granting certain duties in the British colonies and plantations in America," and the preamble proceeded: " Whereas it is expedient that new provisions and regulations should be established for improving the revenue of this Kingdom . . . ; and whereas it is just and necessary, that a revenue be raised, in your Majesty's said dominions in America, for defraying the expenses of defending, protecting, and rearing the same ; . . . we, . . . the commons of Great Britain . . . have resolved to give and grant . . . the several rates of duties hereinafter mentioned."

In view of the recent colonial acquisitions by this country, and the methods adopted for their government, the tenth paragraph is of striking insignificance. It provides that all moneys arising from the

[1] Beer, *op. cit.,* 121.
[2] 4 Geo. III, c. 15. MacDonald, *op. cit.,* 271.

operation of the act, after the expenses of levying and collection were paid, were to be turned into the royal exchequer, to be kept separate from all other funds, and to be "disposed of by parliament, towards defraying the necessary expenses of defending, protecting and securing the British Colonies and Plantations in America." If the Fathers ultimately came to rebel against such a provision, is it any more likely that the colonial Fathers of the future will not be similarly moved? The principle in both cases is the same, and though we may enforce our measures with more tact, they contain elements of grave danger to our political welfare.

The Stamp Act is so well known as to require but brief comment. The main opposition to it was drawn about its revenue clauses. But not the least objectionable of its features was the minuteness of its provisions by reason of which it touched upon the life of the colonists at every point, letting none escape. No man or woman who had business in the courts of law or before an ecclesiastical court, none engaged in trade, none who held public office, none who secured a grant or made a conveyance of land, none who read a pamphlet or an almanac or a newspaper, could fail to come in contact with this tax at some time. The idle were caught in the meshes of its net along with the industrious, for no man could indulge in a game of cards, or hazard a stake at dice, without having this unwelcome token of the power of Parliament rise up to greet him.

Only less irritating than the Stamp Act were the Townshend Acts of 1767, three in number, that establishing customs commissioners, already referred to, the revenue act, known as the "glass, lead and paint" act,[1] and the tea act.[2] As if the taxation feature of the revenue act was thought not to be sufficient to arouse the opposition of the colonists, the last paragraph of this act legalized writs of assistance in the colonies, over which the controversy with England had started in 1761. Thus antagonized, the colonists instituted non-importation agreements, which bore so heavily upon England's merchants that the revenue act was repealed in 1770. Served thus with the first taste of the results of effective opposition to unpalatable enactments, non-importation followed by non-exportation agreements were resorted to in 1774.

When the revenue act of 1767 was repealed in 1770,[3] the duty on tea imported into America was retained, along with the provisions of the tea act of 1767, which granted a remission of the British duties paid on all teas exported to America and Ire-

[1] 7 Geo. III, c. 46, June 29, 1767.
[2] 7 Geo. III, c. 56, July 2, 1767. Both these acts are in MacDonald, 323, 327.
[3] 10 Geo. III, c. 17.

land, and was obviously in the interests of the East India Tea Company. The retention of this duty in 1770, though Americans were enabled to procure tea more cheaply than it could be purchased in England, led to the well-known tea disturbances throughout the country, the most notorious and disorderly of which was the " Boston Tea Party." Elsewhere the landing of tea was opposed with equal efficacy, though not accompanied by such theatrical turbulence. As this tea act expired in 1772, another act was passed in May, 1773,[1] by which the cost of tea in America was still further reduced, but a small tax being retained. Franklin expressed the prevailing opinion when he wrote, " They [the ministry] have no idea that any people can act for any principle but that of interest; and they believe that three pence on a pound of tea, of which one does not perhaps drink ten pounds in a year, is sufficient to overcome all the patriotism of an American."[2]

The wide extension of the jurisdiction of admiralty courts in 1764 (to which were entrusted the enforcement of the Sugar Act), and their increase in numbers in 1768, are responsible for the idea contained in the next charge[3] which is closely re-

[1] 13 Geo. III, c. 44.

[2] *Works,* Sparks' ed., VIII, 49.

[3] " For depriving us in many cases, of the benefits of Trial by Jury."

lated to the succeeding.[1] No cause was ever tried in an admiralty court before a jury, and to authorize, besides, the transportation of offenders for trial was thought to add exile to injustice. Transportation for trial beyond the seas meant the revival of an old law, passed in the reign of Henry VIII,[2] by which it was made possible to send a person, accused of treason in any part of the realm, to England for trial. The first intimation that this act was to be extended to America came in 1769, after the failure of Massachusetts to rescind her Circular Letter, and the riots that took place upon the seizure of John Hancock's sloop, the " Liberty." Parliament early in that year, in an address to the King, made the suggestion that the time was favorable for the revival of the law just mentioned. Matters rested in this uncertain state until June, 1772, when, after the revenue vessel " Gaspee " was burned to the water's edge in Narragansett Bay, the determination to punish violators of the revenue acts, and these destructive rioters in particular, was greatly intensified. A commission was therefore instituted late in 1772 to investigate this offense. These commissioners had extensive powers, yet the weightiest part of their instructions was that which ordered

[1] " For transporting us beyond Seas to be tried for pretended offenses."

[2] 35 Henry VIII.

them to transport the offenders to England for trial.[1]

In the autumn of 1772, just previous to the appointment of this commission, and before the knowledge of the " Gaspee " incident had even reached England, an act had been passed " for the better securing and preserving His Majesty's Dock Yards, Magazines, Ships, Ammunition and Stores,"[2] which included the detested transportation provision. It aroused great opposition, for it deprived the colonists of their dearly cherished right of " a constitutional trial by a jury of the vicinage." The law, already referred to, " for the impartial administration of Justice," while designed to protect the revenue and other officials, also belongs to this category of ills, because of its transportation clauses.

The possible enforcement of the Quebec Act of 1774,[3] with its far-reaching provisions for extending the use of the civil as against the common law, was made the ground of the next grievance.[4]   As it never went into force in any respect, however, it is

[1] Winsor, *Narr. and Crit. Hist.,* VI, 53.
[2] 12 Geo. III, c. 24.
[3] 14 Geo. III, c. 83.   MacDonald, *op. cit.,* 355.
[4] " For abolishing the free System of English Laws in a neighboring Province, establishing therein an Arbitrary government and enlarging its Boundaries so as to render it at once an example and fit instrument for introducing the same absolute rule into these Colonies."

difficult to tell exactly what its effects might have been. Yet the extension of the limits of the province created by the proclamation of 1763, so as to include all the country west of the Alleghanies and south to the Ohio River, meant a further encroachment upon the territory of those colonies that claimed charter rights to much of the land thus included. The reasons already given, therefore, added to the opportunities for further aggression that the enforcement of this act might offer, rendered it one of the laws looked on with the greatest disfavor by the colonists. It appeared to them as but another unwarrantable extension of the royal prerogative, against which they had for so long been contending without avail.

What the Quebec Act lacked in definiteness, however, was more than supplied by the very evident intent of the bill regulating the government of Massachusetts.[1] If any acts of aggression may be set down as the immediate cause of the outbreak of the revolution this and its sister, the Boston Port Act, may be so regarded. None carried with them so much consternation and dismay. None aroused at the same time so much stern opposition. Their great importance, therefore, made it necessary that

---

[1] " For taking away our Charters, abolishing our most valuable Laws, and altering fundamentally the Forms of our Governments."

reference should be made to them in the Declaration. If the power to take away or alter a single charter was once recognized, the rights of no colony were safe from destruction. The principle, if carried to its logical conclusion, meant the possible abolition of all the laws developed by the English in America through a period of a hundred and fifty years, and the substitution in their stead of such manner and form of government as the will of an arbitrary sovereign might dictate. When, therefore, the first-mentioned act[1] abolished, with one stroke, the council as it had been developed; curtailed the power of the assembly; practically put an end to that great institution for the redress of grievances, the town meeting; made serious changes in the manner of selecting the judiciary and jurors; and virtually made the governor the supreme power in the province, we cannot wonder that this act of revenge upon Massachusetts, which foreshadowed what might be expected to happen elsewhere, aroused a spirit of opposition throughout the colonies such as had never before been called forth. Therein lay the main part of the grievance. Yet the earlier decision (1772) to sever the governor of Massachusetts completely from any dependence upon the assembly for his salary, and thereby to make his freedom of action the greater, was also

[1] 14 Geo. III, c. 45. MacDonald, *op. cit.*, 343.

an innovation in settled custom that was viewed with grave disfavor. Also, when the great contest was on in North Carolina, over the establishment of courts, the attempt of the governor to pay no heed to the recalcitrant assembly, by endeavoring to erect courts on his own responsibility, was likewise regarded as " altering fundamentally " an established form of government.

Nor could the colonies ever become reconciled to that short-sighted policy which, because of the spirited resistance of the New York Assembly to the demands made upon it, could offer no other solution of the difficulty than the suspension of the legislature until it bent the knee and yielded.[1] The colonies were accustomed to the exercise of the governor's power of veto and prorogation. This had been submitted to from the beginning, and was regarded as a constitutional mode of enforcing royal authority. But to go much further, and, for so trivial an action on the part of the New York Assembly, as the failure to make what was considered adequate provision for the troops quartered there, to suspend indefinitely its legislative functions by act of Parliament,[2] was regarded as an exercise of

[1] " For suspending our own Legislatures, and declaring themselves invested with power to legislate for us in all cases whatsoever."

[2] 7 Geo. III, c. 59, June 15, 1767. MacDonald, *op. cit.,* 318.

unwarranted authority to which the colonists never became reconciled. Although New York was forced to yield, her cause was made the cause of all, and the voice of protest against this act resounded far and wide. It was, moreover, an enforcement of the Declaratory Act of 1766,[1] little heeded at first, but now seen to be fraught with the utmost danger to colonial rights. By the provisions of that act the imperial crown and Parliament of Great Britain were declared to have conjointly full power to make laws " to bind the colonies and people of America, subjects of the crown of Great Britain, in all cases whatever." And the Tea Acts of 1770 and 1773, were regarded as but other instances of the enforcement of the policy thus announced.

We have come now to the end of the grievances that had their origin previous to the beginning of the armed struggle. For the last five[2] of all the long, unhappy list, the King is once more held to sole responsibility. They have to do with the harsh

[1] 6 Geo. III, c. 12. MacDonald, 316.

[2] " He has abdicated Government here, by declaring us out of his Protection and waging War against us."

" He has plundered our seas, ravaged our Coasts, burnt our towns, and destroyed the Lives of our people."

" He is at this time transporting large Armies of foreign Mercenaries to compleat the works of death, desolation and tyranny, already begun with circumstances of Cruelty & perfidy scarcely paralleled in the most barbarous ages, and totally unworthy the Head of a civilized nation."

events of the beginning of the war—the skirmishes and battles; the proclamation of August 23, 1775, declaring the colonists in rebellion and announcing the intention to suppress the revolutionists with a high hand, and the speech from the throne in October of the same year breathing a like purpose. These led to war in earnest, and with its beginning the royal governors, ever in a perplexing situation, thought it necessary to flee, before the possible disgrace of capture fell to their lot. First Governor Dunmore of Virginia, in June, 1775, soon followed by Tryon of New York, Martin of North Carolina, and Campbell of South Carolina, " abdicated government,"—in the terms of the Act of Settlement of 1689—and left the inhabitants of those colonies to their own devices in creating new forms of government.

The other acts complained of need no explanation, for they all form part of the familiar history of the commencement of the war. The burning of Falmouth and Charlestown, Norfolk and Charleston; the employment of Hessians—" foreign mercenaries "—to fight the cause of England; and the act of Parliament of December, 1775,[1] which authorized the capture and condemnation of trading ships, and compelled " fellow Citizens taken captive on the high Seas to bear Arms against their Country, to

[1] 16 Geo. III, c. 5. MacDonald, *op. cit.,* 392.

become the executioners of their friends and Brethren, or to fall themselves by their Hands,"[1] require no comment to make their meaning clear.

The last grievance[2] refers to a possible condition of affairs, ever dreaded, and against which precautions had been taken by numerous acts of legislation. Those acquainted with life in the South are aware of the fear engendered by the thought of a servile war. Nothing more horrible could be imagined; only the letting loose of bands of well-armed Indians to plunder and devastate the country was to be compared with it. When, therefore, Dunmore, in the spring of 1775, in order to enforce his decrees, threatened to arm negroes and Indians, the alarm created was widespread, and it had much to do with bringing into existence a well-trained militia. The governors of North and South Carolina were known to be adopting similar measures, and the latter was denounced as "having used his utmost endeavors to destroy the lives, liberties and properties of the people." Along with this came the endeavor to en-

[1] " He has constrained our fellow Citizens taken Captive on the high Seas to bear Arms against their Country, to become the executioners of their friends and Brethren, or to fall themselves by their Hands."

[2] " He has excited domestic insurrections amongst us, and has endeavored to bring on the inhabitants of our frontiers, the merciless Indian Savages, whose known rule of warfare is an undistinguished destruction of all ages, sexes and conditions."

gage the Indians as allies, and Gage issued instructions to that effect in the summer of 1775. The Indian agent Stuart, on the borders of South Carolina, made overtures and won to him the Creeks and Chicksaws, while Sir Guy Carleton was making similar progress with the Six Nations in the North.[1]

If impartial consideration be given to the forceful recapitulation of the colonists' contentions in the Declaration, and to the analysis here set down, it must be admitted that the differences were serious, even though some may not regard them as sufficient to warrant recourse to arms. Moreover, they had reason and right,—if not entire reason nor all-convincing right,—to sustain them, amply adequate to justify the course they had pursued. Further, it must be allowed, that if, in the statement of the colonial side, the constitutional right of Great Britain to enact legislation for the government of the colonies is denied, full cause for such denial had been given in the earlier failure to exercise that right. The colonies had been allowed to work out their destinies in their own way with only trifling interference. This was in large measure due to England's neglect to make the most of her colonial possessions on the continent, ignoring them for the wealth that was more easily to be acquired from her West Indian possession. When she awoke to the

[1] Winsor, *Narr. and Crit. Hist.,* VI, Chapter VIII.

17

possibilities lying in the development of the other colonies, the time had passed when they might be put to use mainly for her own advancement. The colonists had learned, during the period of neglect, in what directions lay the opportunities for their own development. They could not abandon them, short of a complete overturn of existing conditions, and to this they would not submit, since they were strong enough to make an effective resistance. Assertion of rights and recital of grievances had been met by determination to enforce submission. Memorials and resolutions appealing to the King, to Parliament, even to the English people, had been put aside and disregarded, or else had been succeeded by measures more obnoxious than those against which protest had been registered. In the Declaration of Rights and the other documents of the first Congress, repeal of practically all the acts, now cited as warrant for breaking off the connection with Great Britain, had been pleaded for in general as well as in specific terms. Every method known to the colonists to bring about the reforms desired had been tried with no results. They had now either to retreat or fight on to victory.

The belief in their own strength, in the righteousness of their cause, is epitomized in the Declaration. The arguments had been made before, and the briefs submitted. The decision was now proclaimed that the time had arrived for them to stand up by themselves in the court of nations, " to acquiesce in the necessity " which caused the separation, and to hold Great Britain, as they held " the rest of mankind, enemies in war, in peace friends." Therefore, as petitions to the King and appeals to the people of Great Britain had proved fruitless of results, there was no other course for them, the " Representatives of the United States of America, in General Congress, Assembled, appealing to the Supreme Judge of the world for the rectitude " of their intentions, than, " in the Name and by authority of the good People " of the colonies to " solemnly publish and declare, That these United Colonies are, and of Right ought to be Free and Independent States ; that they are Absolved from all Allegiance to the British Crown, and that all political connection between them and the State of Great Britain, is and ought to be totally dissolved ; and that as Free and Independent States, they have full Power to levy War, conclude Peace, contract Alliances, establish Commerce, and to do all other Acts and Things which Independent States may of right do." And for the support of that Declaration, with a firm reliance on the protection of Divine Providence, they mutually pledged to each other their lives, their fortunes, and their sacred honor.

APPENDIX

The Declaration of Independence

The Declaration of Independence as drafted by Jefferson, and the engrossed copy, are printed in the succeeding pages for purposes of comparison. The originals are in the Department of State at Washington. The draft reproduced here is the one found among Jefferson's papers when they were acquired by the government. Facsimiles of it are in Randolph's *Jefferson,* and in Ford's, *Writings,* vol. II. This is apparently not the report of the committee, which has not been preserved, but appears to be the draft from which Jefferson may have made the final copy submitted by the committee as its report to the Congress. Jefferson made other copies, one of which is inserted in the manuscript of his *Autobiography,* and another is among the Madison papers, both in possession of the government. Still other copies are among the Richard Henry Lee papers, in the American Philosophical Society (reproduced in facsimile in *Proc.,* vol. XXXVII), the Adams papers in the Massachusetts Historical Society (printed in Ford's *Jefferson's Writings,* vol. II), in the Emmet collection, Lenox Library, and a fragment is in the possession of Mrs. Washburn, of Boston.

The portions of the draft stricken out by the Congress are printed in italics, and those inserted are enclosed within brackets.

JEFFERSON'S DRAFT

A Declaration by the Representatives of the UNITED STATES OF AMERICA, in General Congress assembled.

When in the course of human events it becomes necessary for one people to dissolve the political bands which have connected them with another, and to assume among the powers of the earth the separate and equal station to which the laws of nature & of nature's god entitle them, a decent respect *for* the opinions of mankind requires that they should declare the causes which impel them to the separation.

We hold these truths to be self-evident: that all men are created equal; that they are endowed by their creator with *inherent & inalienable* rights, that among these are life, liberty, & the pursuit of happiness; that to secure these rights, governments are instituted among men, deriving their just powers from the consent of the governed; that whenever any form of government becomes destructive of these ends, it is the right of the people to alter or to abolish it, & to institute new government, laying its foundation on such principles & organising its powers in such form, as to them shall seem most likely to effect their

[In CONGRESS, July 4, 1776. The unanimous Declaration of the thirteen united STATES of AMERICA,]

When in the Course of human events, it becomes necessary for one people to dissolve the political bands which have connected them with another, and to assume among the powers of the earth, the separate and equal station to which the Laws of Nature and of Nature's God entitle them, a decent respect to the opinions of mankind requires that they should declare the causes which impel them to the separation.

We hold these truths to be self-evident, that all men are created equal, that they are endowed by their Creator with [certain unalienable] Rights, that among these are Life, Liberty and the pursuit of Happiness.—That to secure these rights, Governments are instituted among Men, deriving their just powers from the consent of the governed.—That whenever any Form of Government becomes destructive of these ends, it is the Right of the People to alter or to abolish it, and to institute new Government, laying its foundation on such principles and organizing its powers in such form, as to them shall

safety & happiness.   Prudence indeed will dictate that governments long established should not be changed for light & transient causes : and accordingly all experience hath shewn that mankind are more disposed to suffer while evils are sufferable, than to right themselves by abolishing the forms to which they are accustomed.   But when a long train of abuses & usurpations, *begun at a distinguished period, &* pursuing invariably the same object, evinces a design to reduce them under absolute Despotism,[1] it is their right, it is their duty, to throw off such government & to provide new guards for their future security.   Such has been the patient sufferance of these colonies, & such is now the necessity which constrains them to *expunge* their former systems of government.   The history of the present King of Great Britain[2] is a history of *unremitting* injuries and usurpations, *among which appears no solitary fact to contradict the uniform tenor of the rest, but* all *have* in direct object the establishment of an absolute tyranny over these states.   To prove this let fact be submitted to a candid world, *for the truth of which we pledge a faith yet unsullied by falsehood.*

[1] The words " under absolute Despotism " are in Franklin's handwriting, and are in place of the words " to arbitrary power."

[2] The words " King of Great Britain " were substituted by Adams for " his present majesty."

seem most likely to effect their Safety and Happiness. Prudence, indeed, will dictate that Governments long established should not be changed for light and transient causes; and accordingly all experience hath shown, that mankind are more disposed to suffer, while evils are sufferable, than to right themselves by abolishing the forms to which they are accustomed. But when a long train of abuses and usurpations, pursuing invariably the same Object evinces a design to reduce them under absolute Despotism, it is their right, it is their duty, to throw off such Government, and to provide new Guards for their future security.—Such has been the patient sufferance of these Colonies; and such is now the necessity which constrains them to [alter] their former Systems of Government. The history of the present King of Great Britain is a history of [repeated] injuries and usurpations, all [having] in direct object the establishment of an absolute Tyranny over these States. To prove this, let Facts be submitted to a candid world.—

He has refused his assent to laws the most wholesome and necessary for the public good :

He has forbidden his governors to pass laws of immediate & pressing importance, unless suspended in their operation till his assent should be obtained, and when so suspended, he has utterly neglected to attend to them.

He has refused to pass other laws for the accommodation of large districts of people unless those people would relinquish the right of representation in the legislature, a right, inestimable to them, & formidable to tyrants only :

He has called together legislative bodies at places unusual, uncomfortable & distant from the depository of their public records, for the sole purpose of fatiguing them into compliance with his measures.

He has dissolved Representative houses repeatedly & *continually* for opposing with manly firmness his invasions on the rights of the people :

He has refused for a long time after such Dissolutions[1] to cause others to be elected whereby the legislative powers incapable of annihilation, have returned to the people at large for their exercise, the state remaining in the mean time exposed to all the dangers of invasion from without, & convulsions within :

[1] The words " after such Dissolutions " were suggested by Adams.

He has refused his Assent to Laws, the most wholesome and necessary for the public good.—

He has forbidden his Governors to pass Laws of immediate and pressing importance, unless suspended in their operation till his Assent should be obtained; and when so suspended, he has utterly neglected to attend to them.—

He has refused pass other Laws for the accommodation of large districts of people, unless those people would relinquish the right of Representation in the legislature, a right inestimable to them and formidable to tyrants only.—

He has called together legislative bodies at places unusual, uncomfortable, and distant from the depository of their public Records, for the sole purpose of fatiguing them into compliance with his measures.—

He has dissolved Representative Houses repeatedly, for opposing with manly firmness his invasions on the rights of the people.—

He has refused for a long time, after such dissolutions, to cause others to be elected; whereby the Legislative powers, incapable of Annihilation, have returned to the People at large for their exercise; the State remaining in the mean time exposed to all the dangers of invasion from without, and convulsions within.—

He has endeavored to prevent the population of these states, for that purpose obstructing the laws for naturalization of foreigners, refusing to pass others to encourage their migrations hither, & raising the conditions of new appropriations of lands.

He has *suffered the administration of justice totally to cease in some of these states,* refusing his assent to laws for establishing judiciary powers:

He has made our judges dependant on his will alone, for the tenure of their offices and the amount & payment[1] of their salaries:

He has erected a multitude of new offices *by a self-assumed power,* & sent hither swarms of officers to harrass our people & eat out their substance:

He has kept among us in times of peace standing armies *& ships of war* without the consent of our legislatures.

He has affected to render the military, independent of & superior to the civil power:

He has combined with others to subject us to a jurisdiction foreign to our constitutions and unacknowledged by our laws; giving his assent to their acts of pretended legislation, for quartering large bodies of armed troops among us; for protecting them by a mock-trial from punishment for any murders which they should commit on the inhabitants of

[1] The words " and payment " were suggested by Franklin.

He has endeavoured to prevent the population of these States; for that purpose obstructing the Laws for Naturalization of Foreigners; refusing to pass others to encourage their migrations hither, and raising the conditions of new Appropriations of Lands.—

He has [obstructed the Administration of Justice, by] refusing his Assent to Laws for establishing Judiciary powers.—

He has made Judges dependent on his Will alone, for the tenure of their offices, and the amount and payment of their salaries.—

He has erected a multitude of New Offices, and sent hither swarms of Officers to harrass our people, and eat out their substance.—

He has kept among us, in times of peace, Standing Armies without the Consent of our legislatures.—

He has affected to render the Military independent of and superior to the Civil power.—

He has combined with others to subject us to a jurisdiction foreign to our constitution, and unacknowledged by our laws; giving his Assent to their Acts of pretended Legislation:—For quartering large bodies of armed troops among us; For protecting them, by a mock Trial, from punishment for any Murders which they should commit on the In-

these states; for cutting off our trade with all parts
of the world; for imposing taxes on us without our
consent; for depriving us of the benefits of trial by
jury, for transporting us beyond seas to be tried for
pretended offences; for abolishing the free system of
English laws in a neighboring province, establishing
therein an arbitrary government, and enlarging its
bounds so as to render it at once an example & fit
instrument for introducing the same absolute rule
into these colonies; for taking away our charters,
abolishing our most valuable Laws,[1] and altering
fundamentally the forms of our governments; for
suspending our own legislatures & declaring themselves invested with power to legislate for us in all
cases whatsoever:

He has abdicated government here, *withdrawing
his governors,* & declaring us out of his *allegiance &*
protection.

He has plundered our seas, ravaged our coasts,
burnt our towns & destroyed the lives of our
people:

He is at this time transporting large armies of
Scotch and other foreign mercenaries to compleat
the works of death desolation & tyranny already
begun with circumstances of cruelty and perfidy unworthy the head of a civilized nation.

[1] The words "abolishing our most valuable Laws" were
added by Franklin.

habitants of these States :—For cutting off our Trade with all parts of the world :—For imposing Taxes on us without our Consent :—For depriving us [in many cases], of the benefits of Trial by Jury :—For transporting us beyond Seas to be tried for pretended offences :—For abolishing the free System of English Laws in a neighboring Province, establishing therein an Arbitrary government, and enlarging its Boundaries so as to render it at once an example and fit instrument for introducing the same absolute rule into these Colonies :—For taking away our Charters, abolishing our most valuable Laws, and altering fundamentally the Forms of our Governments :— For suspending our own Legislatures, and declaring themselves invested with power to legislate for us in all cases whatsoever.—

He has abdicated Government here, [by] declaring us out of his Protection [and waging War against us].—

He has plundered our seas, ravaged our Coasts, burnt our towns, and destroyed the Lives of our people.—

He is at this time transporting large Armies of foreign Mercenaries to compleat the works of death, desolation and tyranny, already begun with circumstances of Cruelty & perfidy [scarcely paralleled in the most barbarous ages, and totally] unworthy the Head of a civilized nation.

He has endeavored to bring on the inhabitants of our frontiers the merciless Indian savages, whose known rule of warfare is an undistinguished destruction of all ages, sexes, & conditions *of existence.*

He has incited treasonable insurrections of our fellow-citizens with the allurements of forfeiture & confiscation of property.

He has constrained *others* taken captive*s* on the high seas, to bear arms against their country, to become the executioners of their friends & brethren, or to fall themselves by their hand:

He has waged cruel war against human nature itself, violating it's most sacred rights of life & liberty in the persons of a distant people who never offended him, captivating & carrying them into slavery in another hemisphere, or to incur miserable death in their transportation thither. This piratical warfare, the opprobrium of infidel *powers, is the warfare of the* Christian *king of Great Britain determined to keep open a market where MEN should be bought and sold. He has prostituted his negative for suppressing every legislative attempt to prohibit or restrain this execrable commerce. And that this*

He has constrained [our fellow Citizens] taken Captive on the high Seas to bear Arms against their Country, to become the executioners of their friends and Brethren, or fall themselves by their Hands.—

He has [excited domestic insurrections amongst us, and has] endeavoured to bring on the inhabitants of our frontiers, the merciless Indian Savages, whose known rule of warfare, is an undistinguished destruction of all ages, sexes and conditions.

18

assemblage of horrors might want no fact of distin-
guished die, he is now exciting these very people to
rise in arms among us, and to purchase that liberty
of which he *has deprived them, by murdering the*
people upon whom he also obtruded them; thus pay-
ing off former crimes committed against the liberties
of our people, with crimes which he urges them to
commit against the lives *of another.*

In every stage of these oppressions " we have
petitioned for redress in the most humble terms,"
our repeated petitions have been answered only[1] by
repeated injuries.   " A prince whose character is
thus marked by every act which may define a tyrant,"
is unfit to be the ruler of a people *who mean to be*
free. "Future ages will scarce believe that the hardi-
ness of one man adventured within the short compass
of twelve years only" to build a foundation so broad
& *undisguised, for tyranny over a people fostered*
and fixed in principles of freedom.

Nor have we been wanting in attentions to our
British brethren. We have warned them from time
to time of attempts by their legislature to extend a
jurisdiction *over these our states.* We have reminded them of the circumstances of our emigration
& settlement here, *no one of which could warrant so*
strange a pretension: that these were effected at the
expence of our own blood & treasure, unassisted by
the wealth or the strength of Great Britain: that in

---

[1] " Only " added by Franklin.

In every stage of these Oppressions We have Petitioned for Redress in the most humble terms: Our repeated Petitions have been answered only by repeated injury. A Prince, whose character is thus marked by every act which may define a Tyrant, is unfit to be the ruler of a [free] people.

Nor have We been wanting in attentions to our British brethren. We have warned them from time to time of attempts by their legislature to extend [an unwarrantable] jurisdiction over [us]. We have reminded them of the circumstances of our emigration and settlement here. We [have] appealed to their native justice and magnanimity, and [we have conjured them by] the ties of our common kindred to disavow these usurpations, which, [would in-

*constituting indeed our several forms of government,
we had adopted one common king, thereby laying a
foundation for perpetual league and amity with
them: but that submission to their parliament was
no part of our constitution, nor ever in idea of history may be credited; and* we appealed to their native
justice & magnanimity, *as well as to the* ties of our
common kindred to disavow these usurpations which
were likely to interrupt our connection & correspondence. They too have been deaf to the voice of justice
and consanguinity, *& when occasions have been
given them, by the regular course of their laws, of
removing from their councils the disturbers of our
harmony, they have by their free election re-estab-
lished them in power. At this very time too they are
permitting their chief magistrate to send over not
only soldiers of our common blood, but Scotch &
foreign mercenaries to invade & destroy us*[1] *these
facts have given the last stab to agonizing affection,
and manly spirit bids us to renounce for ever these
unfeeling brethren. We must endeavor to forget
our former love for them,* and to hold them as we
hold the rest of mankind, enemies in war, in peace
friends. *We might have been a free & a great
people together; but a communication of grandeur
& of freedom it seems is below their dignity. Be it
so since they will have it. The road to happiness & to
glory is open to us too, we will climb it apart from*

[1] "And destroy us" added by Franklin.

evitably] interrupt our connections and correspondence

They too have been deaf to the voice of justice and
of consanguinity.

[We must, therefore] acquiesce in the necessity,
which denounces our Separation, and hold them, as
we held the rest of mankind, Enemies in War, in
Peace Friends.—

them, and acquiesce in the necessity which denounces our *eternal* separation.

We therefore the representatives of the United States of America in General Congress assembled do in the name & by authority of the good people of these *states reject and renounce all allegiance & subjection to the kings of Great Britain & all others who may hereafter claim by, through, or under them; we utterly dissolve all political connection which may heretofore have subsisted between us & the people or parliament of Great Britain; and finally we do assert and declare these colonies to be free and independant states* and that as free & independant states they have full power to levy war conclude peace, contract alliances, establish commerce, & to do all other acts and things which independant states may of right do. And for the support of this declaration we mutually pledge to each other our lives, our fortunes, & our sacred honour.

We, therefore the Representatives of the united States of America, in General Congress, Assembled, [appealing to the Supreme Judge of the world for the rectitude of our intentions], do, in the Name, and by Authority of the good People of these Colonies, [solemnly publish and declare, That these United Colonies are, and of Right ought to be Free and Independent States; that they are Absolved from all Allegiance to the British Crown, and that all political connection between them and the State of Great Britain, is and ought to be totally dissolved] ; and that as Free and Independent States, they have full Power to levy War, conclude Peace, contract Alliances, establish Commerce, and to do all other Acts and Things which Independent States may of right do.—

And for the support of this Declaration, [with a firm reliance on the protection of divine Providence], we mutually pledge to each other our Lives, our Fortunes and our sacred Honor.

INDEX

slave trade, 216; election
of delegates to, 226.

Congress of 1775–76, con-
vened, 30; responsibilities
of, 30; assumes direction
of colonial affairs, 31;
growth of power and au-
thority of, 32, 33; support
of, by the colonies, 33; effect of the enlargement of
the powers of, 35; em-
phasis of British aggres-
sion the continual policy
of, 36, 41; unconscious
working of, toward inde-
pendence, 37, 38; second
Petition to the King by,
38; rejects Lord North's
plan of conciliation, 39;
adjournment and recon-
vening of, 40; reply of, to
proclamation of King de-
claring rebellion, 41; effect
of proclamation upon, 42,
43; on sending a new petition, 46; proclamation of
Dec. 6, 47; sovereign policy
of, 48; strength of con-
servative in, 50; continued
increase in power and au-
thority of, 51; increasing
strength of radical party in,
59; influence upon, of the
engaging of foreign mer-
cenaries, 67; regulates commercial relations of the
colonies, 68–70, 74; in-
creased power of, 69; on
the question of open ports,
71; opens ports, 73; plans
to secure supplies of war,
74, 75; attributes of, 77;
instructions to delegates of,
77; casts influence on side
of democracy, 80; reaction

in, 81; revolutionary character of, 81, 82; measures
resorted to by, 82; projects
itself into Pennsylvania
politics, 82, 83; antagonism of Pennsylvania As-
sembly to, 83, 85, 86; advocates of independence in,
84; takes measures to show
sympathy with democracy
of Pennsylvania, 86; Maryland feels the hand of, 87;
arrest of Gov. Eden or-
dered by, 87; Maryland
Council of Safety aroused
to opposition to, 88; at-
tempts to overcome inertia
of conservative colonies,
89; recommends local gov-
ernments, 91, 92, 93, 94;
extension of jurisdiction
of, 95; ignores Maryland's
reactionary resolutions, 96;
decides to call for more
troops, 97, 98; Virginia
resolutions to declare independence submitted to, 100,
101; debate on indepen-
dence postponed one day,
102; debates in, on inde-
pendence, 103–106; unim-
portant position of New
York delegation in, 116;
New York delegates to,
given no instructions on
independence, 118–119, 126,
143, 144; on resolutions
for independence, 123–125;
vote of, on resolutions,
125–129; Declaration of
Independence adopted by,
133; state documents is-
sued by, 133, 134; mem-
bers of, who voted for

Declaration of Independence, 142, 143.
Congress, Journal of. *See* Journal of Congress.
Connecticut, radical delegates of, control vote of colony, 58, 59; on independence, 114.
Continental army. *See* Army, continental.
Continental Congress. *See* Congress of 1774; Congress of 1775–76.
Convicts, opposition of colonies to introduction of, 215, 216.
Conway, Moncure Daniel, *Life of Paine,* 55.
Cromwell, Oliver, 208, 243; popular uprisings under, 11.
Cushing, Thomas, letter of, 67.

DEANE, Silas, contract of Congress with, 74, 75; *Deane papers,* 74, 75; in Congress, 84.
Declaration of causes of taking up arms, July 1775, 164.
Declaration of Independence, committee selected to prepare a, 106, 107; draft of, reported to Congress, 121; debate on, 130; omitted paragraphs from draft of, 131, 132; adoption by Congress of, 133; tradition about date of signing of, 134, 135; signing and promulgation of, 134–139; engrossment of, 136, 137; first official reference to signing of, 137; first authentic copy of, with names

of signers, 137; manuscript of, 139; authentication of, 138, 139; date of signing of, 139–149; signers of, 140–149; on the engrossed copy of, 148–149; location of signatures on the engrossed copy of, 150; observance of anniversary of signing of, 151; lack of comprehension of, 152, 153, 159; on the criticism of, 154, 155; criticism of, by John Adams, 156, 157; inherent vitality of, 155, 156; rhetorical side of, 160; denies the right of Parliament to control the colonies, 163; purpose of, 172, 174–177; human elements of, 178; literary form of, 178–180; contemporary opinion of, 180–183; the "unalienable rights" of, 188; upon French origin of, 197; political philosophy of, 200–205; on the right to change form of government, 202, 203; influence of, upon American political institutions, 203; on British supervision over colonial laws, 213, 222; on representation, 222; on the removal and dissolution of assemblies, 224, 225; on naturalization, immigration, and lands, 226, 227; on interference with the administration of justice, 230; on the tenure of office and payment of salaries of the judiciary, 233; on erection of a multitude of offices, 236; on a standing army,

19

Hart, John, 143.
Henry VIII, 249.
Henry, Patrick, 225; on independence, 28, 29.
Hessian troops, employment of, 67, 255.
Heyward, Thomas, Jr., 143.
Hewes, Joseph, 143, 145; North Carolina's interests guarded by, 97.
Hillsborough, Lord, 217, 225; repressive measures of, 9; became first Secretary of state for the colonies, 210.
Hobbes, Thomas, 185, 187, 197; on government, 186; *Leviathan*, 186.
Hooker, Richard, 197; on government, 186, 187.
Hooper, William, 104, 145; member of committee to prepare address against independence, 56; opposes plan of confederation, 104.
Hopkins, Stephen, 142; on rights of the colonies, 14; on government, 195.
Hopkinson, Francis, 143.
Howe, Sir William, proclamation, concerning Boston, 47; at Sandy Hook, 122.
Humphreys, Charles, votes against independence, 129, 143.
Huntington, Samuel, 58, 142.

INDEPENDENCE, first steps toward, 6; not advocated by Congress of 1774, 28; advance toward, 37; not publicly advocated by Congress, 37; popular movement toward, 42, 43; rapid development of sentiment of, 48, 49, 51; motion

against, 56, 57; public sentiment for, 58; preparation for, 61; reluctance of colonists to declare for, 62, 63 and open ports, 71; instructions of five colonies against, 77, 78, 81; attitude of conservatives toward, 79; fight in Congress for, 85; increase in popularity of, 89; status of the sentiment of, the first of June, 1776, 99; motion in Congress for, 100; vote on, postponed one day, 102; debates on, 103–106; vote on, postponed three weeks, 106; New York on, 116; resolutions for, by New York, 120; consideration of resolutions for, 123; debates on resolutions for, 123; vote for, 125–129; denial by colonies of desire for, 166; popular mind prepared for reception of, 199, 200. *See also* Declaration of Independence.
Independence Hall, Philadelphia, 134.
Indians, threat to arm, 256.
Iredell, James, *North Carolina laws*, 231.

JAMES II, 105, 209.
Jay, John, 112; address to the people of Great Britain prepared by, 26; member of committee to confer with New Jersey, 46; on independence, 76, 79.
Jefferson, Thomas, 79, 143, 147, 152, 165, 176, 230, 240, 242; on independence, 28, 29; returns to Congress,

Massachusetts historical society, *Proceedings,* 144, 147.
Massachusetts State papers, 218, 222, 235, 238.
Merriam, Charles Edward, *American political theories,* 186, 197, 205; on sovereignty, 196, 197.
Middleton, Arthur, 143.
Military, independent of civil power, 237, 239.
Milton, John, 186.
Molasses act (1733), 243, 245; (1764), 243, 245.
Montesquieu, Baron, on separation of powers, 198, 204.
Montgomery, General, death of, 57; services in memory of, 59.
Moore, Sir Henry, 217.
Morris, Lewis, 142, 144.
Morris, Robert, 71, 78, 107; on independence, 75, 76, 79, 129; letter of, to Joseph Reed, 129; on the signing of the Declaration of Independence by, 140; opposition of, to Declaration of Independence, 180.
Morton, John, 129, 143, 144.
Mutiny act, extension of provisions of, to the colonies, 238.

NARRAGANSETT Bay, burning of the *Gaspee* in, 249.
Naturalization, generally practiced by the colonies, 228; passage of acts of, prohibited, 229.
Nature, law of, as related to government, 188, 189.
Nature, state of, 186; defined by Locke, 188, 189.

Navigation act (1651), 208; acts, 212.
Negroes, threat to arm, 256.
Nelson, Thomas, Jr., 143.
New England, favors a declaration of independence by Congress, 99; favors the adoption of the resolutions for independence, 104, 105, 125.
New Hampshire, not represented at Stamp act congress, 5; advised by Congress to form a government, 34, 43, 80, 226; appeal of, to Congress for advice on government, 49, 226; on independence, 114; royal instructions to, against opposition to slave trade, 215; on representation, 223, 224.
New Jersey, resolutions of, on non-importation (1774), 19, 20; instructions of, against independence, 45, 77; proposes sending a new petition to the King, 46; contest for independence in, 80; revolutionary changes in, 110, 111; relations of Gov. Franklin and the Provincial Congress of, 111; declares for a new government and for independence, 112; votes for resolutions for independence, 125; laws of, designed to prohibit slave trade, 215; laws of, respecting bills of credit, 218; on representation, 223.
New Jersey Archives, 46, 218.
New Jersey Congress, letter

Sense, 53–55 ; dessemination of *Common Sense,* 61. Paper money, 82. *See also* Bills of credit.

Parliament, acts of, affecting commerce and industries of the colonies, 1, 2 ; projects itself into American affairs, 6 ; beginning of controversy between colonies and, 6 ; remonstrance against authority of, 7, 14 ; opposition of colonies to control by, 162–167 ; establishment of supremacy of, in England, 187 ; attempt of, to revive authority in colonies (1763), 194, 195 ; address King in 1740 upon colonial legislation, 219 ; act of, " for the impartial administration of justice " (1774), 241, 242 ; acts of, on colonial trade (1688–1765), 243, 244 ; act of, authorizing captives to bear arms against their country (1755), 255.

Penn, John, 143.

Pennsylvania, resolutions of, on non-importation (1774), 19, 20 ; attitude toward independence of conservatives of, 43 ; efforts of the conservative party to keep control of government of, 44, 45 ; instructions of, against independence, 45, 77 ; attempt to break up conservative party in, 54 ; radicals of, gain in power, 56 ; reluctance of, to declare for independence, 63 ; Conference of Committees of, 109 ; new instructions of, to dele-

gates, 109 ; dissolution of Assembly of, 109 ; votes against resolutions for independence, 126 ; political situation of, 128 ; votes for independence, 129 ; attempts to overthrow proprietary government in, 162 ; constitution of, 204 ; effort of, to restrict entrance of convicts, 216 ; laws, respecting bills of credit, 218 ; conservative policy of, 78, 79, 90 ; contest for independence in, 80 ; antagonism of Assembly of, to Congress, 83, 85, 86 ; attempt to overthrow the Assembly of, 94 ; protestations of inhabitants of Philadelphia against the Assembly of, 107, 108 ; change of form of government of, 108, 109 ; on independence, 108–110, 128, 129 ; inhabitants of, protest against competency of the Pennsylvania Assembly, 107, 108.

Pitt, William, on the Declaratory act, 15.

Political organizations, intercolonial, 4.

Poore, Benjamin Perley, *Charters and constitutions,* 204.

Ports, opening of, 62, 69, 70, 71 ,73, 78.

Pownall, Thomas, on royal instructions issued to governors, 222 ; *Administration of the colonies,* 222.

Privateering, authorization of, 73, 84.

" Prohibitory Act," 78, 244.

Property, conception of, by